A Curriculum and
Resource Handbook

Seminary Education and Christian-Jewish Relations

Seminary Education and Christian-Jewish Relations

A Curriculum and Resource Handbook
by
Dr. Eugene J. Fisher

Secretariat for Catholic-Jewish Relations
National Conference of Catholic Bishops
Consultor to the Vatican Commission
for Religious Relations with Judaism

Published by
The National Catholic Educational Association
Seminary Department

in cooperation with:
The American Jewish Committee
and
The Secretariat for Catholic-Jewish Relations
National Conference of Catholic Bishops

Washington, D.C., 1983
Second Edition 1988

This publication has been made possible by a grant from the Nathan Appleman Institute for the Advancement of Christian-Jewish Understanding of the American Jewish Committee.

FOREWORD, 1988 EDITION

The five years since the publication of the first edition of this handbook have been extraordinarily rich in substantive (and controversial) developments in Jewish-Christian relations. The Holy See, the World Council of Churches, the U.S. and Latin American Catholic Bishops Conferences (NCCB, CNBB, and CELAM), and numerous Protestant denominations, such as the Lutherans, Presbyterians, Episcopalian, and United Church of Christ have all issued major doctrinal statements and practical guidelines reflecting and fostering progress on all levels from the local to the international. Important scholarly and popular-level works in the field here proliferated in seemingly geometric progression (see additional bibliography, p. 78).

In retrospect, the past half-decade may be viewed as the most significant in the field since the Second Vatican Council.

This new edition, rather than attempting a general overview of these many documents, focuses on an analysis of one catholic document of immediate significance for the work of seminary and theological educators, the (1985 Vatican) *Notes on the Correct Way to Present Jews and Judaism in Preaching and Catechesis* (USCC Publ. No. 970) and the catechetical, homiletical and pastoral implementing documents it has already precipitated in the United States (see new Chapter V, below).

As with the substantive, theological portions of the text, the acknowledgment (p. 11) also need to be updated. Along with Ms. Judith Banki, now Associate Director of the Interreligious Affairs Department of the American Jewish Committee, I would like to thank IAD's new director and my dear friend, Rabbi A. James Rudin. Together, we have weathered many a controversy of the moment and, I like to believe, at the same time have contributed to the ongoing progress of the dialogue (see our book, *Twenty Years of Catholic-Jewish Relations*, Paulist Press, 1986). IAD's many seminary programs, co-sponsored with Catholic, Protestant and Jewish Seminaries around the country, have helped to make this handbook a living tool rather than simply more unheeded words on paper.

Gratitude also needs to be expressed as well to Fr. Charles Kavanagh, he has so ably succeeded Msgr. Baumgaertner in the Seminary Education Department of the NCEA, and also to the Nathan Appleman Institute for its continuing support. Thanks also to the Robert M. Fisher Foundation of Washington, D.C. for its smaller, yet very timely assistance. Finally, I would like to use this opportunity to thank my secretary, Mrs. Levon Monroe, who is leaving the Secretariat for Catholic Relations after fifteen years of untiring service, and Bishop Francis Mugavero of Brooklyn, Episcopal Moderator for the Secretariat for almost two decades, who has been succeeded in that post for the Bishop's Committee on Ecumenical and Interreligious Affairs by Bishop William H. Keeler of Harrisburg, PA.

To both of these colleagues, whose quiet work has been crucial to the effort of the Secretariat, and whom I shall miss greatly, I say *Ad Multos Annos*!

Eugene J. Fisher
Washington, D.C.
April 1988

Table of Contents

Appendices

A. Vatican Council II Declaratin on the Relation of Church to Non-Christian Religions *(Nostra Aetate)* October 28, 1965.
B. 1974 Vatican Guidelines
C. John Paul II, Address to the Jewish Community (Mainz, 1980)
D. John Paul II, Address to Representatives of Episcopal Conferences (Rome, 1982)
E. Archbishop John R. Roach, "A Renewed Vision of Catholic-Jewish Relations" (March, 1981)

Introduction

"Our common spiritual heritage is considerable. Help in better understanding certain aspects of the church's life can be gained by taking an inventory of that heritage, but also by taking into account the faith and religious life of the Jewish people as professed and lived now as well." (John Paul II, Rome, March 6, 1982)

n 1982, the National Association of Diocesan Ecumenical Offices (NADEO) issued the study, *Educating for Unity: A Survey of Ecumenical and Interfaith Education in Catholic Seminaries in the U.S.* Questioned separately in the survey were the rectors, spiritual directors, field educators, and deans of each of the 53 responding seminaries, as well as 70 diocesan vocation directors across the country. The result, in the study's own words, was "an inventory —by no means complete—of the efforts in Roman Catholic seminaries to educate those in training to become priests in their ecumenical and interfaith responsibilities." The data, in sum, revealed both good news and bad:

It seems that the seminary faculty takes seriously the Vatican II mandate that ecumenism should be a context for all theological and ministerial training. But... there are some strains. Perhaps most important of all, there is a gap between the formal recognition of the importance of ecumenism and interfaith matters and its practice.

Though a majority of Catholic seminaries had "occasional" lectures by Jewish scholars," few were engaged in any sort of conversation or exchange arrangement with Jewish institutions or had a part-time Jewish faculty member. Almost none had Jewish students or Jewish full-time faculty, though the opportunity for such contacts with Jews during the seminary years was ranked high by the rectors on their lists of "helpful" and "important" elements in interreligious training. Relatively higher percentages, on the other hand, were reported for elective courses in "Judaism and Jewish-Christian Relations" (40%) and for the study of official statements and the insight to contemporary biblical scholarship within the context of the existing curriculum (75%). Fewer, again reported any effort to track the history of post-biblical Judaism or make use of Jewish spiritual resources such as rabbinic literature (45%). Even less (32%) reported curriculum components on the history of Christian antisemitism without which, it may be said, Christians will have a difficult time understanding the attitudes and approaches to contemporary problems of our Jewish partners in dialogue.

The NADEO survey provides a mixed picture in terms of the implementation in priestly formation programs of the mandates of the Second Vatican Council and subsequent documentation. This picture, however, must be assessed within its proper historical context. As the report concludes, the seriousness of the educators and the amount of activity thus far "represents for Roman Catholicism a degree of contact strikingly different from pre-Vatican II seminary training."

It must be acknowledged, further, that the official teaching itself, as this handbook will show, is only now itself in the process of development, with many complex and nuanced theological questions still unresolved. Seminaries, on the other hand, represent ideal places for raising these issues and applying to them the urgently needed theological and pastoral skills represented by the faculty and students of these central institutions of Church life.

This handbook has sought to provide a resource for the seminaries in their ongoing struggles with the manifold implications of Jewish-Christian relations for all areas of the seminary curriculum. It seeks to do this within the context and restraints of the existing curriculum. Hence it advocates, not so much the introduction of new courses into the "already crowded" curriculum of the contemporary seminary, but rather the integration of insights and components from the dialogue and contemporary scholarship into the existing areas of study, spiritual formation and field education.

The process of development of this handbook has been a long and careful one, going back now for several years and through several drafts. The project originated in conversations between the Secretariats for Priestly Formation and Catholic-Jewish Relations of the National Conference of Catholic Bishops. Early drafts, prepared by the Secretariat for

Catholic-Jewish Relations, were sent to several persons active in seminary education for criticism and comments. A revised draft was then sent, at the suggestion of the Bishops' Committee for Priestly Formation, to a team of leading Catholic Biblical scholars for critique. At this point too, reactions from Jewish scholars were solicited through the Interreligious Affairs Department of the American Jewish Committee.

The resulting (third) draft was sent for comment in March of 1981 to all Catholic seminaries in the U.S. by the Seminary Department of the National Catholic Educational Association in the form of one of its "Seminary Papers." At this stage the reactions of prominent Protestant and Jewish, as well as Catholic scholars were solicited. The resulting suggestions and criticisms have been integrated, it is hoped adequately, into this final revision, which is put out under the auspices of the Seminary Department of the National Catholic Educational Association, in cooperation with the Advisory Committee of the Secretariat for Catholic-Jewish Relations and the American Jewish Committee.

Grateful acknowledgement is here made by the author to all of those whose comments and critiques, sometimes harsh but always to the point, have assisted this long process, especially to Msgr. William Baumgaertner of the NCEA and Rabbi Marc H. Tannenbaum, National Interreligious Affairs Director of the AJC and Ms. Judith Banki of the AJC, who have patiently read and re-read every draft. Acknowledgement is also made to the Nathan Appleman Institute for the Advancement of Christian-Jewish Understanding of the American Jewish Committee for financial assistance in publishing this final draft.

It is hoped that this handbook, which raises more questions than it seeks to answer, will serve as a useful resource tool for the ongoing work of the faculties and students of Catholic seminaries. Though it is addressed primarily to them, it is the belief of all of us who have been engaged throughout the process, that it may be of use in the context of Protestant and Orthodox seminaries, as well in the context of other forms of training for Christian ministry in the Churches. And it might be said to offer something of a challenge, too, to Jewish institutions, not only in its content, but also in its presupposition that the issues here raised are more than simply two-sided, and that there exist among Jews no less than among Christians misunderstandings of the true nature of the "other" as a complex tradition and faith-community (see E. Fisher, "Typical Jewish Misunderstandings of Christianity," *Judaism*, Spring, 1973, 21-32).

Christians must admit, for their part, that while the Jewish-Christian relationship over the centuries has been two-sided, both as regards to misunderstandings between us and as regards to more positive (though seldom acknowledged) sharings of spiritual insights, the sociological facts at least since the fourth century with the introduction of Christianity as the official state religion of the Roman Empire, are that Christians, not Jews, have been in the position of power, and thus in a position to abuse that power. There remains, then, a certain asymmetry in our two stories which cannot validly be reduced to a simple equation of wrongs done.

There is also to be acknowledged an enduring "asymmetry" in the theological relationship itself. Christianity cannot tell its own story without grappling with its historic roots in the Jewish community. Judiasm, however, can articulate its central vision, if not history, with little reference to Christianity.

This asymmetry, however, is by no means as absolute as some would try to render it. Rabbinic Judaism developed in the same period as did early Christianity, reacting to similar historical circumstances and needs. In a dialogue with Christians, Jews stand to learn much about their own development. Nor can it be forgotten from the Jewish viewpoint that, for better or worse, Christianity represents one of Judaism's primary gifts to the world, as great Jewish scholars such as Moses Maimonides, Jacob Emden, Menachem Hameiri, and, more recently, Martin Buber and Franz Rosenzweig have not hesitated to acknowledge.

Pope John Paul II illustrates the proper attitude of dialogue when he states:

If there has been in the past misunderstandings, errors and even insults in the relations between Catholics and Jews, we must now overcome these with understanding, in peace and mutual esteem...The terrible persecutions suffered by the Jews at various periods in history have opened eyes and disturbed many hearts. Because of this, Christians are on the right path, that of justice and fraternity, when they seek, with respect and perseverance, to find themselves again with their Semitic brothers and sisters gathered around the common heritage (Rome, March 6, 1982).

This handbook hopes to make a small contribution to the efforts of those committed to the path along which we are called today by the Church, the path of mutual understanding and interreligious esteem.

I. Basic Perspectives: Church Teaching Today

The Second Vatican Council's Declaration, *Nostra Aetate*, no. 4, marked a watershed in the long history of the relations between Jews and Christians. In it, the Church Council Fathers sought to remove sources of tragic misunderstandings which for so long scarred that relationship. Further, they sought to provide the basis for a more positive understanding of the mystery itself.

The Council declared as a matter of historical fact, that "what happened in (Jesus') passion cannot be blamed upon all the Jews then living, without distinction, nor upon the Jews of today." The Council thus repudiated any implication of collective guilt regarding the Jews as a people. This teaching restated in an unmistakable way the Church's essential tradition concerning Jesus' death: theologically, the sins of all humanity bear responsibility. "In this guilt are involved all those who fall frequently into sin...*our* sins consigned Christ the Lord to the death of the cross...this guilt seems more enormous in us than in the Jews, since according to the testimony of the apostle: "If they had known it they would never have crucified the Lord of glory; while we, on the contrary, professing to know him, yet denying him by our actions, seem to lay violent hands on him (Heb.6:6 1 Cor. 2:8)." (Catechism of the Council of Trent, Article IV)

By focusing our attention once again on the core of our beliefs concerning the meaning of the Paschal mystery, the Vatican Council has enabled us to shed misconceptions concerning the Jews that had grown up over the centuries about the false notion of collective guilt.

From the time of the Church Fathers, for example, we find sermons that seemed to impute to God a petty will to vengeance. God, it was said, desired to punish the Jews for their alleged "rejection" of Jesus. Origen, for example, comments: "Therefore the blood of Jesus came not only upon those who then lived, but upon all generations who followed thereafter even to the end of the world." (Origen, *Comm. in Matt. Ser.* 124; pg. 13. 1775; cf. Thos. Aquinas, *Summa Theologica* 3. 47, 5). Jewish disasters, such as the destruction of the Temple, and by extension all Jewish suffering, thus came to be seen by some Christians as a sort of inverted proof of Christ's triumph. The American bishops in 1975 referred to such notions and their tragic consequences when they stated:

Much alienation between Christian and Jew found its origins in a certain anti-Judaic theology which over the centuries has led not only to social friction with Jews but often to their oppression. (NCCB, November 20, 1975)

Such "teaching of contempt," it must be reiterated, had no theological basis in Christian doctrine. The Nicene Creed referred simply to Jesus as having been "crucified under Pontius Pilate." Yet the deicide charge tragically retained widespread popular appeal. Not only did it provide a comforting rationalization for what was seen as an embarrassment over continued Jewish existence after the coming of Christ, but it also led many Christians, despite official attempts such as that of the Council of Trent, to project onto the Jews their own sinful responsibility for the death undergone for their sake by Jesus. It was conveniently forgotten by many of these preachers that only by assuming that awesome responsibility for Jesus' death are we as Christians enabled to rise with Him in glory.

Once the underlying issue of collective guilt was effectively removed, however, the remainder of the "teaching of contempt" began to fall of its own weight. The Second Vatican Council began the challenge of what the American bishops called in 1975 "the reformation of Christian theological expositions of Judaism along more constructive lines," calling upon us to probe anew what constitutes the authentic mystery of the relationship between our two communities. To begin this process, *Nostra Aetate* relied heavily on St. Paul's major treatment of the question in his Epistle to the Romans, declaring with the Apostle that the Jews "remain most dear to God because of their fathers, for He does not repent of the gifts He makes nor of the calls He issues (cf. Rom. 11:28-29)."

Here, the Council centers our search on the fact of the living continuity of the Judaism of today with that of the Bible. This does not resolve all the exegetical difficulties raised by the several attitudes toward Judaism reflected in various strata of the New Testament (see below). But it does provide us with a key perspective for our ongoing reflection. The 1975 Statement on Catholic-Jewish Relations of the National Conference of Catholic Bishops comments:

In effect we find in the Epistle to the Romans (Ch. 9-11) long-neglected passages which help us to construct a new and positive attitude toward the Jewish people. There is here a task incumbent on theologians, as yet hardly begun, to explore the continuing relationship of the Jewish people with God and their spiritual bonds with the New Covenant and the fulfillment of God's plan for both Church and Synagogue. To revere only the ancient Jewish patriarchs and prophets is not enough...(NCCB, November 20, 1975)

The sense of continuity referred to here needs to be carefully understood. On one hand, it represents a central teaching receiving today increasing attention and clarification. Pope John Paul II, in his remarkable address to the Jewish community of Mainz in November of 1980, referred to the Jews as "today's people of the covenant concluded with Moses" and "the people of God of the Old Covenant never revoked by God," indicating a strong assertion of the permanent validity of the covenant between God and the Jewish people. This central, but much obscured truth of Catholic teaching has, as we shall see, implications for every area of Christian thought, from evangelization to eschatology, which call for careful consideration in the seminary classroom. To give just one example, when the Pope, in calling for a renewed catechesis concerning Jews and Judaism in his address to representatives of Episcopal conferences on March 6, 1982, referred to the "common heritage" that links Jews and Christians "at the very level of their own proper identity," he made clear that this heritage is to be found, not only in the past or in our shared biblical books, but equally through the whole course of our parallel and often interacting spiritual developments up to today. Thus, the living "faith and life of the Jewish people" today, in the Pope's vision, bears witness to Christians, just as Christians and Jews are called, together, to witness the world. Such insights profoundly challenge the way many of us have commonly construed the Jewish-Christian relationship in the past (cf. Appendix for these statements and commentary).

On the other hand, this continuity of the Jewish people in their covenant with God cannot be seen as a reality frozen in time. As the articulation of a living relationship with the Creator, Judaism has developed, changed and been continuously adapted in differing circumstances over the centuries, just as has the Church itself. It would be a grave mistake to perceive the situation as if the Jews alone have maintained a continuity with the Hebrew Scriptures while Christianity represents a break with them (discontinuity). The reality is much more complex and nuanced than that.

Many Christian and Jewish scholars looking at the evidence today would recognize that the Judaism that emerged after the destruction of Jerusalem in 70 of the first Christian century was, as one has commented "as different from the Old Testament and pre-70 Judaism as Christianity is itself." That is to say, neither rabbinic Judaism nor the nascent Church represent replications of biblical Judaism but are, in fact, developments of it. Both rabbinic Judaism and Christianity find their roots and inspiration in the Hebrew Scriptures (and so are inexorably linked to each other), but each represents a distinct growth, a new shoot, as it were, from the common stock. To assent that either is "closer" to those roots than the other (or more authentically "biblical," etc.) would be to sink once again to the level of invidious comparison which caused so much trouble between our two communities in the first place. The point, it needs always to be remembered, is not who is "most dear" to God. In the Christian vision, we acknowledge that both the Church and Jewish people stand in covenant relationship with the Creator. The point, rather, is what God has called us both, Jews and Christians, to do in and for the world. The issue is the building of God's Kingdom, not what place either of us feel we can claim within that Kingdom.

Rabbinic Judaism, no less than Christianity, is a creative development of biblical Judaism. How to worship in community after the loss of the Temple, for example, posed no less of a crisis for developing rabbinism than it did for developing Christianity. And distinct, if often remarkably parallel religious solutions were found by each group in their meditations upon and probings of the common scripture for guidance. Rabbinic Judaism fulfilled the mandate of calling the people to be a "priestly people" by, for example, opening to one and all obligations regarding food and cleanliness originally intended only for the priesthood in preparation for Temple service. Christianity centered on the priestly function of Christ, and on the community's participation (ultimately sacramental) in that function, as in the Epistle to the Hebrews. Paralleling Jesus' dicta on "when two or three of you are gathered together" in the New Testament is a series of sayings in the first tractate of the much later Babylonian Talmud:

How do you know that if ten people pray together the Divine Presence is with them? For it said: 'God stands in the congregation of God.' And how do you know that if three are sitting as a Court of Judges the Divine Presence is with them? For it said: 'Then they that feared the Lord spoke with one another, and the Lord hearkened and heard.' ...And how do you know that even if one man sits and studies Torah the Divine Presence is with him? For it said: 'In every place where I cause my Name to be mentioned I will come unto you and bless you.' (Berakoth, 6a, Soncino transl.)

Such sayings, of course, stand in continuity with the biblical vision, as does the New Testament saying. But they likewise represent a distinct development from that tradition, indeed, a radically new sort of "Judaism" that requires a modifier, "rabbinic" to signal its new as well as its continuous elements. The rabbinic insistence on Oral Torah, a tradition handed down from Sinai but not set in writing until Talmudic times, is clear evidence as the helpful phrase of Jewish scholar Ellis Rivkin points out that a religious "revolution" is underway in such teachings.

Talmudic passages like the above are immersed in and flow from the Hebrew Scriptures according to a distinct, rabbinic methodology which can also be found in places in the New Testament. They represent a distinctive style and pattern of reasoning that is not found as such anywhere in Scripture, but is a response to new challenges and changing situations of the people of God. Adaptability, of course, itself continues biblical tradition. *Chronicles* is a creative *midrash* on, or re-telling of, earlier historical stories told in the Bible, and the later Elohist and Priestly traditions often significantly alter within the Pentateuch itself versions of stories told in the earlier Yahwist saga.

One needs to recognize that just as the diverse and developing movements of the first and subsequent centuries of Jewish thought continued to influence Christian development, liturgically as well as theologically, so would it be invalid to view rabbinic Judaism as having developed in isolation from Christian influence. This point, which is only now beginning to receive the scholarly attention it deserves, will be probed in a bit more (if still inadequate) depth in the New Testament section, below, along with the question of the dating of early Christian and contemporary Jewish sources.

In the meantime, it is important to note, first of all, the call to a wholly new and more positive approach to Jews and Judaism that has emerged from the Conciliar declaration and subsequent affirmations.

The 1974 Vatican Guidelines and other documents particularly invite Catholic institutions of higher learning and priestly formation to participate in this effort, both by making these issues an important element throughout their curricula and by training priestly candidates for their role in interpreting and leading the dialogue from the Catholic side.

The mystery to be probed in this dialogue is as potentially enriching as it is challenging. The Holy Father, in speaking to representatives of the Jewish community around the world, repeatedly stresses the "spiritual bond" which links the Church in its central mystery to the mystery of Israel. Exclusively negative formulations of this relationship are today seen to be inadequate to the reality they attempt to express. We can no longer evade the deeper issues by declaring that the first covenant has been simply abrogated by the New, or that the New has replaced or "superceded" the Old. The "spiritual link" binding Jews and Christians is a present reality, not a past one.

Drawing this out in some detail, the 1974 Vatican Guidelines affirmed that "the history of Judaism did not end with the destruction of Jerusalem, but rather went on to develop a religious tradition. And although we believe that the importance and meaning of that tradition were deeply affected by the coming of Christ, it is still, nonetheless, rich in religious values." Within this perspective, many older formulations and models need to be restructured; for example, the ancient catechetical practice of opposing Judaism and Christianity as if they were polar opposites: "The Old Testament and the Jewish tradition founded upon it must not be set against the New Testament in such a way that the former seems to constitute a religion of only justice, fear and legalism, with no appeal to the love of God and neighbor; cf. Deut. 6:5 Lev. 19:18; Matt. 22:34-40" (Vatican Commission for Religious Relations with the Jews, Dec. 1, 1974). Just as it is the same God who is the author of both Testaments (Dei Verbum 16), so it is the same God who has elected both the Church and the Jewish people.

In 1973, the bishops of France attempted to articulate a renewed vision of the mystery of the relationship between Church and Synagogue in terms of the Jewish tradition of *Qiddush haShem* ("Sanctification of the Name"). They saw this tradition as a possible "content" for Judaism's continuing role in God's salvific design. Again, this was only a beginning, and major difficulties remain. After two millennia of virtual silence between our two communities, we have much to do, as the 1974 Vatican Guidelines remind us, "to learn by what essential traits the Jews define themselves in the light of their own religious experience." "To tell the truth," the Guidelines continue, "such relations as there have been between Jew and Christian have scarcely ever risen above the level of monologue. From now on, real dialogue must be established."

Just how great a price we have paid for the earlier estrangement is illustrated by the American bishops' 1975 statement

Christians have not fully appreciated their Jewish roots...Most essential concepts in the Christian creed grew at first in Judaic soil. Uprooted from that soil, these basic concepts cannot be perfectly understood... Early in Christian history a de-Judaizing process dulled our awareness of our Jewish beginnings. The Jewishness of Jesus, of his mother, his disciples, of the primitive Church, was lost from view. That Jesus was called Rabbi; that He was born, lived and died under the Law; that He and Peter and Paul worshipped in the Temple—these facts were blurred by the controversy which alienated Christians from the Synagogue. (NCCB, Nov. 20, 1975).

This resource handbook attempts to give those involved in priestly formation some sense of the many areas of Catholic life and spirituality that can be enriched by reclaiming such basic "facts" of our faith as those referred to above by our bishops. Because the dialogue is new and the task of re-integrating positive attitudes into the structure of our beliefs "as yet hardly begun," this booklet can best be seen as tentative and exploratory, a catalyst within the existing curriculum for the creative imagination of those who use it.

II. Academic Areas: Attitudes and Understandings

A. SACRED SCRIPTURE

This section seeks to raise only a few of the inter-connected questions concerning Christian-Jewish relations that pertain to biblical studies. Many of these have arisen in formal dialogue between our two communities; others flow from the field of biblical scholarship it self. All of them have implications far beyond themselves into other fields of academic theological study and pastoral practice.

These suggestions should in no way be seen as final resolutions of complex issues. Rather, they are offered as discussion starters for faculty and student consideration.

1. The Hebrew Scriptures

a. The Relationship Between the Testaments

It is the same God, 'inspirer and author of the books of both Testaments, ' (Dei Verbum, 16), who speaks both in the old and new covenants. (1974 Vatican Guidelines)

It can be appreciated on reflection that the view Christians take of the age-old question of the relationship between and relative merit of the two Testaments will deeply influence Christian perception of the relationship between the Church and the Jewish people. For the manner in which the internal Scriptural relationship is construed will determine to a great extent how we understand the ongoing relationship between the two "covenant communities" whose origins the two testaments record and witness to.

Overemphasis on "discontinuity," as has been seen many times in the past, can lead to a false dichotomizing of what is, from the Christian point of view, the one Word of the One God. Such tendencies were already carried to their illogical extreme in the second century by Marcion, whose *Antitheses* posited a virtual confrontation of opposites between the Scriptures.

Lesser examples of the same tendency can be found even today when, for example, Christian commentators so stress the "originality" of Jesus' teaching that appreciation of its context within the Hebrew Bible and contemporary Jewish thought is lost.

Overemphasis on "continuity," on the other hand, can vitiate the integrity of both Judaism and Christianity as distinct, yet essentially interrelated, religious developments. Such tendencies can be discerned, for example, when the typological or Christological approaches subsume all other interests in the text. Here can be lost the sense of the original meaning of the text as God's word to the Jewish people in a particular time and place, as well as the sense of its value on its own grounds as the living word of God addressing us directly today (cf. *Dei Verbum*, 4).

The question is hermeneutical as well as exegetical. Openness to dialogue with Jews on the meaning of Scripture for them, can greatly assist the students' efforts to achieve the type of balance called for by the 1974 Vatican Guidelines in which "both Old and New illumine and explain each other," as should the religious communities which hold them sacred.

Pope John Paul II makes clear that the relationship, both between the Church and the Jewish people and between the Hebrew Scriptures and the New Testament, is best understood, not as dichotomy but as a dialogue of mutual esteem:

The first dimension of this dialogue, that is the meeting between the people of God of the old covenant never retracted by God (Rom. 11:29), on the one hand, and the people of the new covenant on the other, is at the same time a dialogue within our own church, so to speak, a dialogue between the first and second part of its Bible. (Mainz, Nov. 17, 1980)

Viewing the question this way can shed exciting new light on traditionally intransigent problems, such as the proper theological stance to take toward the relationship between the testaments. Catholic biblical scholar, Joseph Blenkinsopp, in a critical study of the ongoing crisis on this point in the attempts of Christian scholars to develop a "theology of the Old Testament," concludes:

If the general impression conveyed in this essay is overwhelmingly negative, and if we have said little positively about the relation between Old and New Testament, we can only plead that we are as yet nowhere close to knowing how to write Old Testament theology. It seems that first we must take Tanakh seriously on its own terms which, given the way it came into existence, involves coming to terms with the Second Temple period inclusion of early Christianity as a phenomenon of Second Temple Palestinian Judaism. It involves further, as a necessary consequence, coming to terms historically and theologically with Judaism which, far from declining or disappearing at the time of early Christianity, only reached its most characteristic expressions several centuries later...I would argue that the relation of Christian faith to the Old Testament and, by extension, to Judaism is central to the agenda of Christian theology today. (J. Blenkinsopp, "Tanakh and New Testament," in L. Boadt, et al., eds., *Biblical Studies: Meeting Ground of Jews and Christians*, Paulist, 1980, 113-114).

b. Its Own Perpetual Value

The Vatican Guidelines, relying on *Dei Verbum* 14 and 15, comment that "an effort will be made to acquire a better understanding of whatever in the Old Testament retains its own perpetual value." Neither the Guidelines nor *Dei Verbum* spell out the exact extent of this crucial "whatever." That remains a matter of much debate within Judiasm as well as Christianity, though from differing perspectives in each. Neither religion, for example, practices any longer the Temple sacrifices detailed in the Pentateuch, a fact which places an interesting (and limiting) perspective on the comments concerning the early Israelite (perhaps desert) cult described in the Epistle to the Hebrews. The Epistle to the Hebrews is thus not so much a commentary on the relationship between Judaism and Christianity as such, as it is on "Judaizing" tendencies or a religious development parallel to the (later) rabbinic institution of prayer, study and good deeds as a replacement for the actual practice of the Temple cult.

The presuppositions underlying various schools of biblical scholarship, therefore, should be brought out and examined in the light of current Christian-Jewish understandings. The so-called "evolutionary" reconstruction of biblical history implicit in much of the work of Wellhausen and Harnack, for example, has tended to impose on our understanding of *Heilsgeschichte* a rather simplistic notion that everything later is somehow better than everything earlier in the bible. J. L. McKenzie, in *A Theology of the Old Testament* (Doubleday Image, 1976, p. 341) has recently debunked such simplistic views of the divine "plan" as ascribed to Scripture.

Dialogue with Jews as faithful holders and interpreters of Torah can help to illumine such critical issues. The potential for mutual enrichment will be enhanced to the extent that Jew and Christian respect each other's fidelity to God's Word in our ongoing struggles to discern an authentic way to live up to the divine will. Inviting Jewish scholars as guest or part-time lecturers and requiring Jewish commentaries as secondary source readings will expand the exegetical possibilities which the students perceive, and help avoid misperceptions of the text. Rabbinic Judaism's developing notion of "Oral Torah" and the New Testament's "covenant of the Spirit" (based as the latter is on biblical models in Jeremiah and Deuteronomy) can speak to one another today out of common concerns and common hopes.

c. Terminology

Many of the terms to which we are accustomed have different connotations in Christian and Jewish contexts. There is, for example, no such distinction in biblical Hebrew as that which we make today between "body" and "soul." Likewise, there is no true equivalent in Hebrew for the terms "Law" (Greek, *nomos*) as we apply it to the Pentateuch. *Torah* means "teaching" and the rabbinical term *halachah* means literally "the way" or "the going."

Translating Torah as "the law" can result in an unfairly legalistic view of Scripture. Our normal Christian usage of terms such as Old Testament can also have unfortunate connotations. It can seem to imply that the "new" has replaced the "old" or that the two are somehow opposed to one another in their teachings. In Judaism, the bible can be called *Torah* (by extension from the first five books to which the term primarily refers) or *Tanakh*, a vocalized Hebrew acronym descriptive of its contents: *Torah* (Pentateuch), *Nebi'im* (Prophets), *Ketubim* (writings). Neither of these terms in Jewish usage, of course, would include those portions which we Catholics accept as canonical from the Septuagint (e.g., Judith, Tobit, Sirach, Baruch, 1-2, Maccabees), but which were not included in the Masoretic canon accepted by rabbinic tradition in the second century. To posit on *Tanakh* a name, "Old Testament," not recognized by the Jewish community, whatever the validation for the practice within Christian tradition, would not seem the best way to exemplify the spirit of "mutual esteem" to which we are called today.

There is, in point of fact, strong precedent in the New Testament for the phrase "new covenant" (Heb. 8:13 10:16-17; 1 Cor. 11:25; 2 Cor. 3:6), from which "New Testament" derives by way of the Latin Vulgate. While the phrase "old covenant," finds precedent in Hebrews 7:23 and 2 Cor. 3:7-18, other terms for what the apostolic writers accepted as "God's Word" (Heb. 4:12) can also be found. 2 Tim. 3:16 and Hebrews 11:5, for example, simply use "Scripture." Hebrews 8, which concludes with the statement that "what has become obsolete and has grown old is close to disappearing (Heb. 8:13), uses the phrase "first covenant" (8:7) in introducing the citation from Jer. 31: 31-34 from which the phrase "new covenant" itself ultimately derives.

While the Temple and its sacrifices have disappeared, however, Judaism as a living religious tradition certainly has not. Like the Hebrew Bible, rabbinic Judaism retains its own "perpetual value" in God's sight. Perhaps, then, the occasional use of such alternate phrases as *Tanakh* or "the Hebrew Scriptures" (though some segments exist only in the Greek) in course designations can help to alert students to the proper dignity of this portion of Scripture and of Judaism itself. As the Vatican Guidelines point out: "The history of Judaism did not end with the destruction of Jerusalem, but rather went on to develop a religious tradition...rich in religious values."

d. Covenants in Context

In an important paper delivered to a meeting of the Vatican Commission for Religious Relations with the Jews in Rome (March 4, 1982), Father Maurice Gilbert, S.J., pointed out that the whole issue of covenants in the Bible needs to be expanded and more delicately nuanced. The reality is not, in fact, a question of "the" old covenant versus a new one, but rather of a series of covenants, each in its way "new" and "unique" with respect to the others, whether chronologically "before" or "after" it.

Even a short list of the biblical covenants, Gilbert maintains, would include the following: the covenant with Noah (Gen. 9:8-17), the covenant with Abraham (Gen. 15 and 17), the Sinaitic covenant (Ex. 24), the covenant with David (2 Sm. 7), the priestly covenant (Nb. 25:10-13, cf. Mal. 2:4-5; Jer. 33:21; Neh. 13:29), not to mention the "new" covenant described by Jeremiah (Jer. 31:31-34). Each of these covenants, Gilbert notes, has its own proper characteristics and unique revelatory features. The later ones (chronologically speaking) do not preclude or replace the earlier, but add new facets to the diamond-prism of God's self-giving and caring commitments to, and interactions with, the people called into being and challenged to grow through them.

In such a context, the biblical scholar is able to speak of the newness and uniqueness of the covenant in Christ without falling into simplistic "either/or" and "before/after" models of the divine/human relationship. The Christ event maintains its full integrity and universal implications without necessitating a polemic against other events in sacred (which is to say divine/human) history. Taking increasing importance in such a perspective, of course, are often-neglected theological notions such as the "economy of the Spirit." It is too soon to tell, perhaps, how such studies will work themselves out in detail, but the challenge and potential do seem to exist within such approaches for a renewed biblical as well as systematic theological understanding of God's Word.

e. Unfair Appropriation and the Quest for Uniqueness

Quite often, in catechesis and homilies, various ethical and spiritual values which originate in the Hebrew Scriptures and are reflected in the New Testament are "appropriated" and presented as Christian teachings. While it is fair, in one sense, to do this since such values are, in fact, Christian ones, it is not fair to present them without acknowledgement of the Jewish origins of the teachings. One example which was often (mistakenly) called "the new law of love" is that of Jesus' response to the question, "Which is the first of all the commandments?" (Mk. 12; Lk. 10; Mt. 22). Jesus' answer cites directly from Deuteronomy 6:5 and Leviticus 19:18. Here, as in many such instances, a study of the full text from which Jesus cites can add immeasurably to the student's understanding of the saying (cf. E. Fisher, *Faith Without Prejudice*, Paulist, 1977, 33-35).

Another example, this time from a recent religious education text, will serve to illustrate the unfortunate dynamic involved. It is a tendency to subsume Jewish into Christian thought that appears in more sophisticated form in many graduate-level texts:

For a certain person in a certain place, in a certain time, Judaism may be the best religion... However, Christianity remains the best objectively for three reasons:
1. Christianity is built on love, not fear;
2. Christianity teaches that the whole person is good, both the body and the spirit;
3. Christianity teaches that each person is free to be uniquely him or herself.

Obviously, all three of these religious insights flow from the Hebrew Scriptures (e.g., Dt. 6:5; Gn. 1, 4-7). The last, interestingly, represents a teaching of Torah centered on and profoundly developed by Pharisaic-rabbinic teaching along much the same lines as that of Jesus (cf. J. T. Pawlikowski, O.S.M., *Christ in the Light of the Christian-Jewish Dialogue*, Paulist Stimulus, 1981, 76-107). It is one thing for Christians, in faithfulness to revelation, to accept Jewish teachings as their own; it is quite another to attempt to appropriate Jewish thought as "uniquely" Christian and then use it to attempt to "prove" Christian superiority over Judaism.

Indeed, it may be that the whole enterprise of trying to find Jesus' teaching "superior" or "unique" vis-a-vis Jewish thought contains a fatal flaw. The point, one would presume, should not be how unique Jesus was over against other Jewish teachers of his time, but whether or not what he taught was authentic and valid. The quest for the "distinctive" elements of Jesus' teaching may be an interesting and useful study, but taken to extremes, it became a diversion from the main issue of our religious quest, i.e. understanding Jesus' essential message. Unique aspects there certainly are, as with any great teacher or thinker, but mere originality says little about how central such elements may have been to the teacher himself. Indeed, exclusion of and concentration on such features may in the long run only serve to divert attention from what *is* of central significance.

f. Tanakh as Torah

Understanding the Hebrew Scriptures as *Torah*, divine teaching transmitted and applied by a community to its daily life over almost a millenium of its history, opens up rich spiritual possibilities not easily available to students who are taught to approach the biblical Old Testament text primarily as "Law" *(nomos)* or as mere background to the New Testament.

The New Testament cannot be properly interpreted without the Hebrew Scriptures and the history of the Church that extends from the end of the Apostolic age to our own contemporary times. There is, simply put, no such thing as "uninterpreted" Scripture or a disembodied, contextless Word of God. There can be great value, therefore, in seeing in the Hebrew Scriptures, as in Church history, an "interpretation model" of how everyday life and in the larger human scene God's ideals can be implemented and followed.

One can think here of God's "commixeration" in refracting divine hopes through human earthly means. In contradistinction to the almost mechanistic notion of "progress" so prevalent in Western throught since the beginning of the industrial age, the "divine plan" as sketched in Jewish Scripture represents anything but a neat, "later is better" or linear model. God is portrayed by the Yahwist author of Genesis 2, for example, as bringing animal after animal to "the man" in vain search for an "equal opposite" for him, until finally the divine is "taught" by the human that only a true equal "helpmeet" of his own flesh will do. And Abraham, Moses, and Zipporah, among others, are all able by quick wit to modify stated divine actions. The divine Planner "repents" of creation itself and constantly seems to be forgetting, remembering, pursuing, plotting and generally pulling metaphorical rabbits out of hats to keep the "plan" moving along. The eschaton, in such a context, is a goad to as well as the goal of human history. It is the category of the eternal present, not simply the "logical" result of a chronological, step by step process toward the future. Something of this biblical serendipity of the divine / human relationship, one would suspect, needs to be kept in focus when hearing Jesus' proclamation to us out of his Jewish context that the Kingdom (an active, verbal notion, not a static nominal) is "at hand."

Therefore, as Father Carroll Stuhlmueller, C.P., has written, "while the New Testament so often presents the pure ideal which must always be kept in mind, the Hebrew Scriptures, extending over a far larger period of time, place us in a position to gain more practical directions for implementing God's ideals." The Hebrew Scriptures enable us to see the interaction of religion and culture across many centuries of time. They enable us to see a continuity in revelation and yet also to recognize how God's ideals are always implemented in and through the local cultures of particular places and times. At any moment of the Hebrew Scriptures it is almost, if not actually impossible, to disentangle the divine ideals from the human understanding.

The Hebrew Scriptures also afford us an opportunity to see the interaction between what might be called fringe or peripheral ideas and main theological thrusts. For instance, universal salvation to some extent remained a peripheral sort of notion through much of the Hebrew Scriptures, yet from the Christian point of view, this fringe idea would be seen as actually a kernel or, in Stuhlmueller's words, a "heart for the future" for Christianity as it evolved out of biblical Judaism.

Finally, because of its long period of development and almost numberless authors, the Hebrew Scriptures are truly a work of "the people of God," with an immense variety of individuals and groups bringing their own distinctive "joys and hopes, griefs and anxieties" to the proclamation itself. Particularly in the Psalms, we can see how popular piety interacts with the central theological and liturgical expressions of a living religion, affording the opportunity to witness how popular ideas contain within themselves some of the most important theological developments in the history of Israel's religion.

2. The New Testament

...that they will understand the true interpretation of all the texts and their meaning for the contemporary believer...especially when it is a question of those passages which seem to show the Jewish people in an unfavorable light (1974 Vatican Guidelines).

Ever since *Divino Afflante Spiritu* (1943), communication of a sense of the historical setting and an ability to understand individual passages within the context of the Gospel message as a whole have been central to New Testament courses in Catholic seminaries. These dynamics are crucial as well for the student's ability to achieve a proper understanding of the complex reality that was First Century Judaism. The list presented here is not exhaustive but illustrative of the types of considerations that need to be discussed if students are to take full advantage of the insights flowing from contemporary scholarship and dialogue.

a. Anti-Judaic Polemics in and Jewish Context of The New Testament

That the New Testament authors, in varying degrees and from differing viewpoints, engaged in polemical attacks on the Jews and Judaism of their time cannot be denied. The picture that one receives of the Pharisaic movement from the invectives gathered together in Matthew 23, for example, is an exceedingly harsh one, and if taken as a full portrait of developing Pharisaism, would be wholly inadequate. Matthew's gospel does not intend to present the type of dispassionate presentation of Judaism which we would expect in our own textbooks today. It is not history at all in the modern sense, but a proclamation of the good news, more concerned with the values and meanings of events than with the events themselves. It is, in short, *kerygma*, not journalism.

To attempt to derive an adequate understanding of Judaism from the gospels alone would be fruitless endeavor. Apologetic and polemic, while valid on their own grounds and within their own context, should never be confused with objective descriptive writing—especially when the subject concerns a group with whom the New Testament authors were in intense religious competition for potential converts. Below are given some general suggestions which may be of help in framing an approach to the anti-Judaic polemical strata of the New Testament.

(1) Before attempting to formulate these suggestions, a short note on the rather complex questions of dating and dependency may be in order. This handbook assumes the general chronology of the texts in so far as there is a scholarly consensus on such matters. For the New Testament texts, this would presume dates from the 40's and 50's of the first century for the earlier epistles, and from the 70's to the turn of the century for the gospels. The gospels should not be considered eyewitness accounts. Each went through various stages and complex strata development, especially liturgical, before being set down in the form we know them today. With regard to the polemic edge of New Testament writing, therefore, it is often (not always) possible to discern a "development" from less harsh to harsher attitudes toward Jews and Judaism. In some cases, less harsh and more open approaches postdate earlier views, depending on the theological thrust and sociological setting of a particular book or passage.

Episcopalian scholar John Townsend, for example, has traced attitudes toward Jews based on normally accepted stages of the literary development of John's Gospel. In the sources usually considered by scholars to reflect earlier stages of the Gospel's development, Townsend finds remarkably positive attitudes toward Jews and a generally acceptive attitude toward Jewish belief and practice. "Salvation is of the Jews" is here not to be taken lightly. One message to be gained from such data, then, is that the proclamation of the good news does not need to be presented in an anti-Jewish way. The good news can be, as it was in early times, proclaimed in a manner quite positive toward Jews and acceptive of central Jewish religious affirmations.

In the last stages of John, however, Townsend discerns increasing bitterness toward Jews and a developing "rejectionist" theology concerning Judaism. This incipient *adversos Judaeos* tradition in John reflects, of course, the situation in which it developed, in the immediate wake of the "divorce" between evolving rabbinic Judaism and at least the Johannine community. Townsend concludes:

Unfortunately, the anti-Jewish teaching of the Fourth Gospel did not stop with its final redaction. John soon became one of the most influential writings in the early Church, and its popularity has continued to the present day...Today, we may learn to understand the anti-Jewish tenor of the gospel as the unfortunate outgrowth of historical circumstances. Such understanding in itself, however, will not prevent the gospel from continuing to broadcast its anti-Jewish message unabated (in A. T. Davies, ed., *Anti-Semitism and the Foundations of Christianity*, Paulist, 1979, p. 88).

Here it might be noted as we shall affirm again below, is where the job of the exegete ends and the task of hermeneutics, of preaching and catechesis, begins, or, perhaps better, the point of contact and dialogue between exegete and theologian. All too often the later theological speculations and applications of biblical materials, especially those of the Patristic Age, are projected back unto the New Testament text itself, reducing the latter's complexities and nuances to absolute condemnations, not supportable by the text itself in its original context.

(2) A second matter concerning the question of dating needs to be raised at the outset of this section. It will be argued here that the Jewish sources need to be used along with Patristic and other traditional sources in order to understand the full context of New Testament attitudes toward Jews and Judaism. The use of Jewish sources has been gaining in importance for New Testament scholars (thankfully) for some time now, particularly since the discovery along the shores of the Dead Sea of the Scrolls of the Qumran sect. These scrolls were written, roughly, during the same period in which the New Testament was developed. So their ap-

plicability as background for understanding the Judaism of the first century is apparent. The writings of Philo and Josephus, though perhaps somewhat removed in provenance and style, are also chronologically pertinent to New Testament studies.

Less apparent in their applicability, however, are other Jewish sources such as *midrashim*, *targumim*, and rabbinic literature (Targum, Tosefta, etc.), which were set down only in the centuries following the close of the Apostolic period. These sources, of course, reflect long oral (and, in the case of the targums, liturgical) stages, which overlap the New Testament period and in certain cases may well predate the time of Jesus by decades or even centuries. The process of dating the stages of development of rabbinic literature, however, is enormously difficult, as the many works of Jewish scholar Jacob Nuesner illustrate. Individual sages or rabbis mentioned in the text (if and when sayings are so attributed, of course), can sometimes be dated with some security. Far less secure, however, are the sayings themselves even when so attributed. And the particular nuance or thrust of the saying in which the New Testament scholar is interested may, even then, reflect one or another stage of its transmission. Extreme caution, therefore, is always indicated in the use of Jewish sources not certainly datable to New Testament times.

One example of the responsible use of such materials (and one eminently suitable for use in the seminary classroom as an introductory text) is R. LeDeaut's *The Message of the New Testament and the Aramaic Bible (Targum)* put out by the Biblical Institute Press (Rome, 1982). Works by such Catholic scholars as J. Fitzmeyer, S.J., D. Harrington, S.J., and M. McNamara can also serve as models. LeDeaut's work contains an excellent bibliography for targumic studies.

The Talmud which, beginning with the *Mishnah* was set down from the second to the sixth centuries (depending on what one includes) also represents a valuable source for understanding the Jewish context of Jesus' teaching and early Christian thought. For one recent example on a particularly rich point of contact, see J. Swetnam, S.J., *Jesus and Isaac: A Study of the Epistle to the Hebrews in the Light of the Akedah* (Rome: Biblical Institute, *Analecta Biblica* 94, 1981).

Obviously, however, questions of dependency (who "took" what from whom) will not be very profitably pursued given such wide time gaps and complexity of dating. Rabbinic material, on the other hand, can be very suggestive and often corrective, as we shall see, of common Christian misconceptions concerning the enormously rich and vital thought-world of first century Judaism. In *Faith Without Prejudice* (Paulist, 1972), for example, E. Fisher argues not that Jesus' teaching was dependent upon or equivalent to that of the (often later) rabbis, but that, it normally "fit" well within the rather wide parameters of internal Pharisaic-rabbinic disputes. Such parallels and similarities between Jesus' teaching and the later teaching of the rabbis need to be used to understand Jesus within his own Jewish context. They will, and should, quickly disabuse students of the stereotypical and false notion that Jesus' teaching can be understood apart from or "over against" developing rabbinic Judaism in general and Pharisaism in particular.

Regarding "dependency," it also needs to be affirmed (and more carefully studied) that Jesus' teaching may have had more influence on developing Pharisaic-rabbinic teaching than either Jews or Christians have been willing to admit (for opposing apologetic reasons) up to the present time. This situation is now gradually beginning to change. Rom. 15:8 names Jesus as a servant *(diakonos)* of the Jewish people and growing numbers of Jewish scholars, such as Israelis David Flusser and Pinchas Lapide are increasingly able to "reappropriate" the contributions of Jesus' teaching to and within Jewish thought. The New Testament records several instances, such as that concerning plucking grain on the Sabbath, cited below, where Jesus' ruling on a case anticipates conclusions ultimately reached by the rabbis. Another case would seem to be that of the interpretation of the biblical Lex Talionis (cf. E. Fisher, "*Lex Talionis* in the Bible and Rabbinic Tradition," *Journal of Ecumenical Studies*, Summer, 1982; 582-587). Basic thrusts of Jesus' teaching, such as the emphasis on the spirit of the law, direct address to God outside the context of the official Temple cult, etc., also gained prominence within developing rabbinism (though, again, the question of dependency may prove impossible to establish today).

Rabbi Asher Finkel of Seton Hall University's Department of Judaeo-Christian Studies notes in a recent article, "Yavneh's Liturgy and Early Christianity" *(Journal of Ecumenical Studies*, vol. 13 no. 2, Spring, 1981) that "the development of *Halakah* (rabbinic law) at Yavneh reaches similar conclusions as those taught by Jesus" on such matters as the harlot's hire (Luke 7:37-8:3; *Midrash Hagadol* to Dt. 23:19) and on healing on the Sabbath *(Mekhilta* to Ex. 31:13). Regarding the former, the Palestinian Talmud is quite explicit in stating that "one of the disciples of Jesus the Nazarene," by the name of Jacob, recounted Jesus' dicta on the question to Rabbi Eliezer, who was "pleased" with it, though later felt he may have gotten into trouble because of that (Finkel, *op. cit.*, 247-249).

Various sections of rabbinic literature and Jewish liturgy likewise appear to have developed in creative response to the challenge of Christian claims (for examples, see M. Chernick, "Some Talmudic Responses to Christianity, Third and Fourth Centuries," *Journal of Ecumenical*

Studies, Summer, 1980; and B. Z. Bokser, "Religious Polemics in Biblical and Talmudic Exegesis," *Journal of Ecumenical Studies*). One example will suffice to give the flavor of such defensive rabbinic alterations of Jewish tradition. Where the Bible, with God speaking in the first person, states simply: I led you out of the land of Egypt," the Passover *Haggadah* reads: *ani velo malach* ("I am not a messenger..."), which would seem to be in response to Christian claims concerning Jesus' role and Moses as a prefiguring or "type" of Jesus.

There was, then, continuing fertilization of Judaism from Christianity just as there continued to be fertilization from rabbinic Judaism to Christianity. Justin Martyr's *Dialogue with Trypho* and Origen's *Contra Celsum*, in their own apologetic ways, each testify to such phenomena. Even Chrysostum, whom Catholic historian Frederick Schweitzer not unjustly calls "an antisemitic volcano" gives back-handed testimony to the continuing influence of Jewish on Christian thought in his diatribes against those of his congregation who preferred the rabbis' sermons to his own. If Jews and Christians continued to study Torah together even at that late date, certainly the image we now have of two communities so fundamentally opposed as to be wholly isolated from and insulated against each other is an erroneous one.

(3) It should, as has been shown above, be remembered that the New Testament texts reflect the times *in* which they were written as much as they reflect the times and events of Jesus' life. This principle is especially important in dealing with the gospel narratives and Acts. In many cases which seem to show sharp dichotomies between Jesus' views and those of his contemporaries, examination may substantially alter the judgment of the original events involved.

Many of Jesus' sayings and rulings on matters of the "Law," for example, have startlingly close parallels within rabbinic literature. While the *Mishnah*, the earliest portion of the Talmud, was not edited from its earlier, oral sources until the end of the second century (thus prohibiting direct use for analytic purposes), the overall impact of such parallels indicated that Jesus' teaching may not have been as fundamentally opposed to Judaism or to the "religious establishment" of his day as many Christians have previously assumed. The works of Christian scholars such as E. P. Sanders, *Paul and Palestinian Judaism* (Fortress, 1977); E. P. Sanders, ed., *Jewish and Christian Self-Definition* (2 Vols., Fortress, 1981); J. Parkes, *Theological Foundations* (Vallentine-Mitchell, 1960); G. F. Moore, *Judaism in the First Centuries of the Christian Era* (3 Vols., 1924; Schocken reprint, 1971); G. Sloyan, *Is Christ the End of the Law?* (Westminster, 1978); K. Stendahl, *Paul Among Jews and Gentiles* (Fortress, 1976); F. Mussner, *Traktat uber die Juden* (Kosel-Verlag, 1979); L.

Boadt, ed., *Biblical Studies* (Paulist Stimulus, 1980); and C. Thoma, *A Christian Theology of Judaism* (Paulist, 1980) can help to correct many misunderstandings.

One suggestive example among many others may help make this point more concrete. In Mt. 12:1-8 (Mk. 2:23-28; Lk. 6:1-5) Jesus' disciples are censured by the "Pharisees" for plucking ears of "corn" on the Sabbath and, in Lk. 6:1, rubbing them with their hands. The *Mishnah (Shabbath* 7,2), however, lists only "winnowing and grinding" as acts of labor which would violate the Sabbath rest. Would the disciples' action as described constitute a matter that should have brought down upon them the concerted ire of "the" Pharisees? The Babylonian Talmud shows that rabbinic opinion was divided even in a much later period: "One may pluck with the hand and eat, but one may not pluck with an implement; and one may rub and eat, but one may not rub with an implement." These words are attributed to Rabbi Akiba (2nd Century), but other sages say that one may rub with one's finger-tips and eat, but one may not rub a quantity with the hand (and eat)." (*Shabbath* 128ab; see M. McNamara, *Targum and Testament*, Eerdmans, 1972, 9). Opinion might well have been divided among the Pharisees of the first century as well. Or it may have been that an earlier ruling was later mitigated in rabbinic Judaism precisely along the lines Jesus indicated. In any case, the polemic edge of the New Testament passage in terms of Jewish-Christian relations is ofter significantly modified by a study of Jewish sources taken on their own grounds.

(4) The obvious fact must be remembered that the New Testment is not a single book set down all at once with a single philosophical or theological point of view. The seeds of many different potential "theologies" of Judaism, stemming from different needs in different stages of its development, are contained within it. No single attitude for today can easily be deduced from its pages. If, in the past, the negative has been emphasized almost exclusively as binding on the Christians in their treatment of Jews, a new, more positive balance must be sought today (cf. 1975 NCCB Statement).

The deeper issue here is as much one of hermeneutics as it is of exegesis. In what way do we say today, for example, that Christ, who personally lived the "Law" and upheld it as staunchly as any Pharisee (Mt. 5:17-19), is its end (Rom. 10:14)? Such questions cannot be resolved by choosing one text over another, but only by a basic reassessment of the underlying message of the gospels vis-a-vis the living Jewish people in Jesus' time and, not incidentally, in our own.

The study of parallel texts can provide excellent opportunities for illustrating the variety of viewpoints within the New Testament. One such passage is the giving of the Law of Love (Mk. 12; Lk. 10; Mt. 22). In both Mark and Luke, Jesus is approached by a single questioner, who approves his answer and is in his turn praised (Mk. 12:34; Lk. 10:28). Jesus' response is taken from the Hebrew Scriptures (Dt. 6:5; Lv. 19:18), and is typical of rabbinic dicta on the same theme. The Matthean version, on the other hand, written in the context of what appears to have been a rather bitter struggle, perhaps between some in Matthew's community and certain of the local rabbis, significantly alters earlier versions of the story. Now it is "the Pharisees... assembled in a body...in an attempt to trip him up" who pose the question. A scene of amity has become one of confrontation reflective more of events taking place in Matthew's time than Jesus'.

(5) The hermeneutical question here raised is not unique to Christian-Jewish issues. Various moral dilemmas are encountered in reading the Bible, all of which is given us "for our salvation" *(Dei Verbum,* 11). Is the polemical view of Judaism found in the New Testament binding on the Christian conscience today any more than is the apparent approval of holy war in the Deuteronomic tradition or the institution of slavery in 1 Cor. 7:21-11? The apostolic writers certainly could not have envisioned that their words, written at a time when the Church was tiny and powerless, would be put to such a devastating use as they were by later generations of Christendom.

(6) The context and intent of New Testament passages must always be clearly delineated. While in some cases, the intent is to indict "the Jews" in general for their "failure" to accept Christian teaching concerning Jesus (as occasionally in the Gospel of John), in other cases the polemics are more circumscribed in their intended recipients. To apply to all Jews of all times what was intended for a more limited audience would be to misinterpret seriously the original text. Peter's discourse in Acts 4, for example, was aimed not at the people as a whole, but at the "leaders of the People! Elders!" (4:8), whereas, "the people" are described as holding the Apostles in "great esteem" (5:13).

Likewise, the extent to which St. Paul's various comments on the "Law" *(nomos)* are intended to be an assessment of Judaism as such needs to be carefully considered. In context, the central question with which Paul seems to have been grappling was that of a defense for his "gospel to the uncircumsized" (Gal. 2:7; cf. 1:15f.; 2:2) rather than the spiritual validity of the Torah for Jews. "By what logic do you force the Gentiles to adopt Jewish ways?" (Gal. 2:14), Paul demands of Cephas, proceeding to argue that "God's way of justifying the Gentiles would be through faith" (Gal. 3:8; cf. Gn. 12:3), rather than the "Law."

Paul would seem to affirm the continued election of the Jewish people (Rom. 3:1; 9:3-5; 11:28f). He seldom cites any of the standard rejection texts such as Is. 6; Ps. 118, (but cf. Rom. 11:8) and appears only once to have applied the name "Israel" to the Church (Gal. 6:16) as "the Israel of God." While Paul will speak against the claim of anyone who would put observance of the "Law" before faith in Christ, his primary aim seems to have been to provide a rationale for the inclusion of Gentiles in God's plan without the necessity of their prior conversion to Judaism. "For we hold that a person is justified by faith apart from observance of the Law. Does God belong to the Jews alone? Is he not also the God of the Gentiles?" (Rom. 3:28-29). This argument, for Paul, by no means necessitates abolishing the validity of Torah for Jews, as he himself affirms (Rom. 3: 30-31). (See L. Gaston, "Paul and the Torah" in A. T. Davies, ed., *Antisemitism and the Foundations of Christianity*, Paulist, 1979, 48-71).

(7) General stereotypes need to be broken down. While John's gospel seldom makes adequate distinctions among "the Jews" (cf. M. Lowe, "Who Were the Ioudaioi?" *Novum Testamentum* 18, 1976, 101-103; and J. Townsend, "The Gospel of John and the Jews" in A. Davies, ed., *Antisemitism and the Foundations of Christianity*, Paulist, 1979, 72-79), the student will need to keep them uppermost in mind. In Acts, the Sadducee party is clearly intent on supressing the Apostles by whatever means necessary (e.g., 5:17). Pharisees, however, rise to the Apostles' defense (5:33-41; 23:6-9). Luke uses a similar pattern in his passion narrative as well, where the Temple party plots against Jesus while Pharisees seek to save his life (Lk. 13:31).

For a helpful summary of recent views on Luke materials, see the dialogic essays by Rev. Gerard Sloyan and Rabbi Pinchas Lapide in "The Parting of the Ways: Rabbinic Judaism and Early Christianity," in *Face to Face: An Inter-religious Bulletin* (Vol. IX, Spring 1982), 3-16. For a summary of views on John's Gospel and a challenging view of his own, see Sloyan's "Israel as Warp and Woof in John's Gospel" in the same issue. Sloyan summarizes his discussions of Lowe's study of John's use of *Ioudaioi* with the following:

The one exception in John to *hoi ioudaioi* as Judeans rather than Jews in general is Chapter 4. There we have reflected the Samaritan usage of the period and not the Palestinian Jewish usage...In conclusion, "Jews" is probably a correct translation at 4:9 (twice) and 4:22 (and) at 18:20 ("in the Temple where all the Jews congregate"). It is likewise allowable at 6:41, 52. In every other case, it should be "Judeans."

Some think that a discussion like that reported above is rooted chiefly in a concern for contemporary Jewish-Christian relations and resist it because of its suspect scholarly motives. In fact, the evangelists' terminological intent is the best reason to pursue the inquiry, not any modern relief provided by translations that could be dismissed as doubtful. Present trends in scholarship incline toward the view that John's concern with the community of his day is uppermost and the events of Jesus' life secondary *(ibid.*, 19).

It is with concern for such questions that the 1974 Vatican Guidelines note:

There should be an overriding preoccupation to bring out explicitly the meaning of a text, while taking scriptural studies into account. Thus the formula 'the Jews' in St. John, sometimes according to the context means 'the leaders of the Jews' or 'the adversaries of Jesus,' terms which express better the thought of the evangelist and avoid appearing to arraign the Jewish people as such. Another example is the use of the words 'pharisee' and 'pharisaism' which have taken on a largely perjorative meaning.

b. Antisemitism In and Proclamation of the New Testament

The presence of polemic in the New Testament should not mislead the student to conclude that the gospels are antisemitic in the modern sense of the term. This would be anachronistic. As E. Flannery has shown *(Anguish of the Jews*, Macmillan, 1965), anti-Jewish attitudes were widespread before the rise of Christianity (see J. L. Daniel's summary of the evidence in JBL [1978] 45-65). Modern antisemitism is a phenomenon essentially distinct from, though historically related to, Christian theological polemics (see "Church History," below).

The classical, pagan anti-Jewishness of the Roman writers was characterized more by xenophobia than by racist ideology as we now know it. Jewish insistence on belief in only One God was perceived by the Romans as a strange and potentially dangerous sort of religious and political posture. Because of Jewish refusal to worship the Emperor or participate in the official state cult, Jews were seen at one and the same time as "atheists" and as politically treasonous. Such negative pagan attitudes toward Jews were brought with them into the Church by the gentiles who joined the Church after the apostolic age. Many of the great Christian writers, such as Pope Gregory the Great, had classical educations as lay persons, which inevitably tinctured the attitudes they brought with them to the reading of the New Testament. Ignorant of the Jewish context of the New Testament writings the negative gentile attitudes were gradually crystallized into theological absolutes until, with the writings of St. John Chrysostum, we arrive virtually at "the complete antisemite," with attitudes of hatred so deep as to condone severe forms of persecution and violence, all in the name of the God of love!

Still, as we shall see, such attitudes, reprehensible as they were, did not issue into the genocidal mania characteristic of modern "secular" antisemitism. The most severe legislation of Church law did not appear until the high middle ages (12-13th centuries), even then contenting itself with social and economic oppression rather than mass murder. (The rampages of the Crusaders were not planned by Church policy, though admittedly incited by the preaching of certain clerics and not very effectively fought against by Church leaders.) Racial antisemitism, as we know it today, does not seem to have made an appearance until the infamous "purity of blood" laws of Spain in the 15th and 16th centuries. To project such later developments back unto the biblical authors would obviously be anachronistic.

Yet, the matter must be faced that the polemics against Jews and Judaism embedded in various New Testament strata did prove susceptible, with devastating ease, of providing rationalizations for political opression of the Jews when such was seen as expedient by Christian rulers. And today, with two millenia of abuse of the New Testament message behind us and with religious antisemitism part of our very culture, the hermeneutical and pastoral-liturgical question of how to proclaim the good news in an overwhelmingly antisemitic environment becomes an acute and acutely delicate one.

Various solutions, from a "moratorium" on the liturgical proclamation of certain New Testament passages, to a more careful translation of lectionary readings ("*some* Jews," "*some* Pharisees," etc.) have been offered, all trying to remain true to the letter of the biblical text while freeing its spirit to address us in love as the message is intended. Catholic theologian David Tracy poses the challenge this way:

The painful, repressed memories of Christian antisemitism have also been aided by the anti-Judaic statements of the New Testament, especially, but not solely in the Gospel of John. If these scriptural statements cannot be excised, then minimally, they should always be commented upon whenever used in liturgical settings and noted critically in every Christian commentary on the Scriptures. The history of the effects of those New Testament anti-Judaic outbursts should signal the need for Christians, singly and communally, to reflect upon ways to banish forever this bad side of the good news of the New Testament. Those anti-Judaic statements of the New Testament have *no* authoritative status for Christianity. Even the most "fulfillment"-oriented Christology has no real theological need for them. The heart of the New Testament message—the love who is God—should release the demythologizing power of its own prophetic meaning to rid the New Testament and Christianity once and for all of these statements. (D. Tracy, "Religious Values after the Holocaust," in A. Peck, ed., *Jews and Christians After the Holocaust*, Fortress, 1982, p. 94).

Tracy is not arguing here in any sense for an excision or "bowdlerizing" of the New Testament text, but for what he calls a "Christian hermeneutics of suspicion" vis-a-vis the texts that will in turn make possible a Christian "hermeneutics of retrieval" in the light of what is, indeed, of the essence of the biblical proclamation in both testaments.

New Testament scholar Raymond Brown would seem to be arguing along similar lines when he writes:

(The) context of mutual hostility between the Johannine community and the Synagogue must be taken into account when reflecting on the Johannine passion narration. Today Christians are embarrassed by such hostility...An initial response is one of 'Speak no evil; see no evil; hear no evil,' namely, to omit the anti-Jewish sections from the public reading of the passion narrative. In my opinion, a truer response is to continue to read the whole passion; not subjecting it to excisions that seem wise to us; but once having read it, then to preach forcefully that such hostility between Christian and Jew cannot be continued today and is against our fundamental understanding of Christianity. Sooner or later Christian believers must wrestle with the limitations imposed on the Scriptures by the circumstances in which they were written. They must be brought to see that some attitudes found in the Scriptures, however explicable in the times in which they originated, may be wrong attitudes if repeated today. They must reckon with the implications inherent in the fact that the word of God has come to us in the words of men. To excise dubious attitudes from the readings of the Scripture is to perpetuate the fallacy that what one hears in the Bible is always to be imitated because it is 'revealed' by God, the fallacy that every position taken by an author of scripture is inerrant. (from "The Passion According to John," *Worship*)

Both these statements reflect an awareness of the urgency and centrality of the crisis facing the Church today. Obviously, such forceful preaching (and the careful catechesis and adult education that should prepare the congregation for it) will require a realistic re-alignment of priorities within our educational system as a whole, and especially in the seminary curriculum, if Church leaders are to be prepared adequately for the challenge. In the meantime, however, the problem will continue to worsen, so the responsibility remains an immediate one for liturgists and liturgical translators.

Alan T. Davies, in summarizing the conclusions reached by a dozen Christian scholars called upon to grapple with *Antisemitism and the Foundations of Christianity* (Paulist, 1979) adds this hopeful note to the discussion:

If a common motif in these essays can be discerned, it is the conviction that Christians need to choose between an ideological defense of their scriptures that wards off damaging criticism and the sad conclusion that the New Testament is so wholly contaminated by anti-Jewish prejudice as to lose all moral authority. Instead, through careful study, Christians can isolate what genuine forms of anti-Judaism really color the major writings and, by examining their complex historic genesis, neutralize their potential for harm (xv).

c. Jesus as Jew

Some commentaries, even recent ones, can lose sight of the Jewishness of Jesus and his teachings in what can only be described as over-zealous attempts to establsh a sense of his uniqueness. Some of these, for example, go to such lengths to describe his originality or to distinguish him from the Jewish movements of his time and place that it is hard to discern how he could have been a Jew at all. While there is no evidence to assume that he was a member of any particular sect in a formal sense, it is likely that he interacted with (learning from and in turn influencing) many of the wide spectrum of groups and movements proliferating in his day.

We need to question today the tendency to define Christianity as over against Judaism in all its essentials. Doctrines such as the resurrection of the body, the final judgment, and angels, were shared by Jesus' followers and contemporary Pharisaic circles. Certainly the two religions are distinct. We need to re-assess in what sense it is the *person* of Jesus (as Messiah, as divine) and in what sense it is his *message* that forms the basis of that distinction. The Our Father *(Avinu)*, for example, is wholly Jewish in tone and content. And each of the elements that comprise the Sermon on the Mount can find a parallel within the Talmud. Indeed, as we have speculated above, Jesus' teachings on such matters may themselves have influenced the development of rabbinic thought. In assuming too that the antitheses in the Sermon as reconstructed by Matthew represent matters of dispute between Jesus and Judaism as such, one can do disservice to both.

d. Responsibility for the Death of Jesus

The passion narratives have been subjected to close critical analysis in recent years. The four accounts differ in significant details. Was there a full "trial" at night (Mt., Mk.) or only a brief questioning at dawn (Lk.)? (John includes no "trial" at all.) What was the role of Pilate? In the passion narratives there can be detected an increasing tendency from the earlier to the later gospels to emphasize the role of the Jewish figures (priests, scribes, elders), while exculpating Pilate.

Nostra Aetate stated simply that with regard to the trial and death of Jesus, "what happened in his passion cannot be blamed upon all the Jews then living, without distinction, nor upon the Jews of today."

G. Gloyan, *Jesus on Trial* (Fortress, 1973) surveys the historical and biblical questions. For a variety of views see the collection of nine essays by Christian and Jewish scholars in *Judaism Quarterly* (Vol. 20, no. 1, Winter, 1971), 6-74. See also J. Fitzmyer, "Jesus the Lord," in *Chicago Studies* 17 [1978], 87-90, and *A Christological Catechism: New Testament Answers* (Paulist, 1982); J. Pawlikowski, *Sinai and Calvary* (Benzinger, 1976) 90-98; G. Sloyan, "Recent Literature on the Trial Narratives" in T. J. Ryan, ed., *Critical History and Biblical Faith* (Villanova, Pa. College, Theology Society, 1979) 136-176; H. Cohen's *The Trial and*

Death of Jesus (KTAV, 1977) contains provocative suggestions which will stimulate classroom discussion, though not all positions are acceptable.

e. Cautious Use of Reference Works

Students should be alerted that few reference tools are entirely free of the apologetical conventions that have sadly characterized so much of the relationship between Judaism and Christianity in the past. Rabbi Solomon Schechter's classic *Aspects of Rabbinic Theology* (Macmillan, 1909; Schocken paperback, 1961), for example, was written precisely as a response to what he called "the many strange statements by which the Jewish student is struck when reading modern (Christian) divinity works" (p. 21).

Even such standard Christian reference works as H. Strack and P. Billerbeck, *Kommentar zum Neuen Testament aus Talmud und Midrasch* and G. Kittel's *Theological Dictionary of the New Testament* show a tendency in their selections from available Hebrew and Aramaic materials to allow apologetical needs to act as a filter in their approach to Jewish thought and practice, as Samuel Sandmel pointed out in his 1961 presidential adress before the Society of Biblical Literature ("Parallelomania," *JBL* 31 [1962] 1-13; cf. E. Fisher, "The Use and Abuse of Hebrew Sources in Recent Christian New Testament Scholarship," *Hebrew Studies*, Vol. 21 [1980] 199-208). Balancing Jewish and Christian commentaries on the same subject will take more effort but will reward the student with a fuller pictrure of ancient reality.

E. P. Sanders, in *Paul and Palestinian Judaism* (Fortress, 1977) cites numerous specific examples of "how Billerbeck has distorted the clear meaning of a text or has prejudiced a question by his selections" (p. 42), along the way showing how such eminent New Testament scholars as Rudolf Bultmann have been seriously misled and in turn mislead others, by the uncritical and exclusive use of second-hand sources concerning rabbinic tradition. To cite one, relatively harmless example, Billerbeck lists a targumic interpretation on Dt. 30:11-14 apropos of John 3:13. But, as R. LeDeaut notes *(cit.,* 29), Billerbeck includes only the "first part of the text, the part which refers to the notion of ascending. This prevented him from seeing how he could have used [the whole passage] for Romans 10:6-8." The more serious problem, as E. P. Sanders affirms (p. 58) is that Billerbeck often *makes up* whole beliefs from his own personal prejudices, such as his "Pharisaic soteriology" and, by judicious selection and excision of the material gives his pre-judgments the appearance of being derived from the rabbinic material (Sanders, *cit.,* pp. 56-60). Failure to introduce students to the proper use of rabbinic materials, then, can only leave them unprepared for a critical reading of even the most basic scholarly works being written about the New Testament, for even today the influence of Billerbeck and Kittel remains pervasive in Christian scholarly circles.

f. The Pharisees

From what has already been seen, it should be becoming clear that the Pharisees have tended to receive something of a "bum rap" in Christian literature, including scholarly studies, up to the present day. The Pharisees, in fact, were not universal "bad guys" or un-regenerated hypocrites. Rather, they seem to have fought religious hypocrisy much as Jesus did. In contemporary Jewish and later rabbinic accounts, which are themselves often guarded in reference to them, the Pharisees are seen as religious innovators respected by and closer to the people than the aristocratic Sadducees. To the strict letter of the law, the Pharisees opposed the notion of Oral Torah, which allowed for the adaptation of the biblical mandates to changing needs of the people.

The Pharisaic movement was anything but the monolithic, lock-step movement one might imagine from an uncritical reading of the New Testament alone. Indeed, Pharisees seem to have delighted in the differences among them and to have brought creative dissension to the level of an art form. The Talmud is almost unique in religious literature in recording not just majority, but minority and even contradictory opinions on every conceivable subject.

Regarding the Pharisees, a famous Talmudic dictum (Ber. 9:7, Sat. 5:7) cites seven distinct classes of Pharisees (cf. E. Fisher, *Faith Without Prejudice, cit.*, 38-39). The first five categories are satirical of religious ostentation, depicting these groups much as Jesus is shown to have depicted them in Mt. 23. There is, for example, the "bruised" Pharisee, who breaks his head against a wall to avoid looking at a woman, and the "pestle" Pharisee, whose head is bent in sham humility like a pestle in a mortar. The sixth category, however, is the "God-fearing" Pharisee, who is like Job. The seventh, and highest in the view of the later rabbis, is "the Pharisee of love," who is likened, in a phrase reminiscent of St. Paul, to Abraham. Again, questions of dependency and dating remain unclear. The point is that for all its weaknesses, the Pharisaic movement did strive to maintain significant religious ideals. Its teachings and beliefs, of all first century Jewish movements appear, as manifested in Jewish literature, closest to that of the Christian movement. Pharisees, as described in Josephus, maintained belief in the resurrection of the body and a final judgment, in angels and human free will, all beliefs fundamental to Christianity and ones which distinguished the Pharisees as a group over against other groups of their time. Perhaps it was their very closeness to nascent Christianity that made the early Church see them and the later rabbis as such a threat. Given the situation as best as we can construct it today, it is unlikely in any event that the Pharisees would have seen in Jesus' teaching much of a threat compared with other Jewish groups with whom they were in often bitter conflict.

John T. Pawlikowski, in his various works, provides several excellent, brief summations of the relations between Jesus and the Pharisees based on contemporary studies (cf. *What Are They Saying About Christian-Jewish Relations*, Paulist, 1980, pp. 93-107; and *Christ in the Light of the Christian-Jewish Dialogue*, Paulist, 1982, pp. 71-107). For Jewish studies, see especially Michael J. Cook's excellent "Jesus and the Pharisees" (*JES*, Summer, 1978, Vol. 15, no. 3, 441-460) and Ellis Rivkin, *A Hidden Revolution* (Abingdon,. 1978). Jacob Nuesner's many works are of critical importance, and disagree with Rivkin's views on significant particulars.

Hostility between Jesus and the Pharisees may have been more apparent than real in Jesus' lifetime, with the bitter conflicts depicted in the later gospels more a reflection of the time in which those gospels were set down than the time about which the New Testament authors are writing. Whether Jesus actually was a "love Pharisee" or not may be impossible to determine on the basis of present evidence, but these Pharisees, among whom Jesus worked and with whom he seems to have engaged in lively debate in their own style, were certainly not alien to him in major beliefs or practices. As John Pawlikowski suggests, such Pharisees, like Jesus, sought to "internalize" the Law in the hearts of the people. They saw in its observance, especially concerning the Sabbath, a primary vehicle for preserving Jewish communal and religious identity in a volatile period of Jewish history. Pawlikowski in *Christ in the Light of the Christian-Jewish Dialogue* summarizes:

In the area of doctrine the resemblances continue. Emphasis on love, on the Shemah, on the themes summarized in the Beatitudes and on the Resurrection indicate the presence of a strong Pharisaic spirit in the life of Jesus. In particular Jesus' stress on his intimate link with the Father picks up on a central feature of Pharisaic thought. Granted that Jesus' personal sense of identification with the Father, as Clemens Thoma insists, went far beyond the degree of linkage between humanity and divinity that the Pharisees were willing to admit. Yet this sense of God-human person intimacy is not wholly new and unique with Jesus, as is usually believed by Christians. It represents an extension, albeit of quantum proportion, of the new consciousness of the God-human person relationship experienced by the Pharisees (p. 93).

g. A Question of Balance

Balance and a willingness to reassess traditional stereotypes in the light of new appreciations are called for throughout the enterprise of interpreting the message of the New Testament for the Christian community today. If the New Testament reveals in many places a decided polemical bias against Jews and Judaism, it must be remembered that the New Testament authors were reflecting their own and their communities' quite natural bitterness at what they felt was an expulsion from the Synagogue sometime after the destruction of the Temple in the Year 70 (e.g. John 9:22; 9:34f; 12:42). This expulsion may have been accompanied by violence (Jn. 16:2-3) and the violent (as well as protective) attitudes of some Jews toward Christians is attested amply in Acts, e.g. in the martyrdom of Stephen (acts 6-8; cf. Lk. 6:22, 21:15-17).

Mention is made in Justin Martyr's *Dialogue with Trypho* (really an apologetic by today's standards) and other early Christian sources (e.g. Epiphanius, *Haereses* 24:9) of continuing Jewish polemical attacks on the Christian movement. Jerome's *Commentary on Isaiah* several times accuses the Jews of cursing Christians "day and night" (cf. his treatment of Is. 2:18; 49:7; and 54:5). Such charges, however, are seldom corroborated in Jewish works of the period. The few references to Jesus in the Talmud are negatively phrased, but the texts are so late and often so confused in their extant versions that it is not clear even whether it is the same "Jesus" being spoken of (cf. TB *San* 43a; *Git.* 56b-57a; *BerR* 98:9). Jesus in some instances is referred to as "the Nazarene," while in other cases there seems to be a confusion with a certain Jesus ben Stada, who was condemned for practicing Egyptian magic at Lydda (see Finkel, *cit.* 248-249; and M. Goldstein *Jesus in the Jewish Tradition*, Macmillan, 1950 pp. 57-62). On Talmudic criticism of Christianity see K. Hruby, *Die Stellung der juedischen Gesetzeslehrer zur Werdenden Kirche* (Zurich, 1971); J. Maier, *Jesus in the Talmud* (Darmstadt, 1977); J. Lauterbach, *Rabbinic Essays* (Cincinnati: HUC Press, 1951) 473-570. On the daily curse against the *minim* ("heretics," "degenerates"), see the nuanced treatment in Clemens Thoma, *A Christian Theology of Judaism* (Paulist, 1980, 146-152). Thoma's conclusion concerning the Talmudic material is worth noting here:

(The few) sayings hostile to Jesus date to the time after the fourth century CE and the changes under Constantine, when the Church in her position as imperial power acted with hostility toward Jews. The Mishnah [second century]...does not contain a single passage clearly denouncing Jesus or Christianity. At a time when the Church Fathers loudly and aggressively preached and wrote against the Jews, such refraining from polemics is proof of considerable inner strength. (p.89)

The question of whether the curse on the *minim* introduced into the 18 Benedictions by the rabbis of Yavneh (post 70 C.E.) was intended to exclude Jewish Christians from the Synagogue, or whether the *minim* represented a more general category of "heretics" that would necessarily have included Jewish-Christians remains undecided and the subject of much scholarly inquiry. The fact that the much later versions of the 18 Benedictions found in the Cairo Geniza felt it necessary to add *nosrim* (Nazarenes) to the earlier reference to *minim* would seem to indicate that *minim* did not originally include Christians, who were only added later, perhaps after the time of Constantine when Christians had begun actively to persecute the Jews of the Roman Empire. Likewise, the fact that Christians continued to attend synagogues in large numbers (and that Christian leaders continued to complain about it) would indicate that most, if not all, synagogues remained open to Christians long after the presumed "expulsion" in the first century.

Finkel's study, "Yavneh's Liturgy and Early Christianity" (JES, Spring, 1981) and R. Kimelman's "*Birkat Ha-Minim* and the Lack of Evidence for an anti-Christian Jewish prayer in Late Antiquity" (in E. P. Sanders, ed., *Jewish and Christian Self-Definition*, Fortress, 1981) both argue strongly that the evidence is simply not there to support the thesis (now a scholarly consensus among many Christians) articulated so convincingly by W. D. Davies in his *The Setting of the Sermon on the Mount* (Cambridge, 1966). D. Hare and P. Siegal, in a position paper on "Yavneh and Jewish Christianity" for a task force on Matthew presented at the August, 1976 meeting of the Catholic Biblical Association, support the notion of an "excommunication" of the Jewish-Christians from the synagogue by means of the *minim* clause, but themselves admit the "hypothetical" nature of key points of the argument. Finkel and Kimelman, on the other hand, after their own independent studies of the evidence, call the thesis "historically untenable." Whatever the conclusion, the controversy provides another example of the caution that must be exercised in the use of rabbinic materials.

While balance is always a goal to be sought in scholarship, a properly balanced view of the tragically polemical relationship between Judaism and Christianity, whether in the first four centuries or in succeeding ages, does not seem to support any simplistic notions of "equivalency" of hostility between Jews and Christians, verbal or physical. And in any case, it is our own house, not that of the Jews, that we Christians have a primary duty to put in order.

Since passages taken from the New Testament have so often been used in the past to justify Christian hostility toward Jews, an "overriding preoccupation" to reassess our understanding of our Christian texts with a renewed spirit of humility is the least that can be called for in biblical coursework today.

An excellent overall text on many of the key biblical questions involved in the dialogue can be found in L. Boadt, H. Croner and L. Klenicki, eds., *Biblical Studies: Meeting Ground of Jews and Christians (Paulist Stimulus,* 1980, $7.95). The text includes nine articles by Jews as well as Christians on such topics as "The Relationship of Hebrew Bible and New Testament" and recent biblical theology.

B. LITURGY AND HOMILETICS

The above considerations of the biblical problematic of the Jewish-Christian reality naturally leads into a discussion of the liturgy. Since an essential role of the priest in the liturgy lies in commenting on the Bible, the liturgical implications of the Scriptural section of this booklet should be readily apparent. Some of these can be briefly summarized in the following "rubrics."

1. *Affirm the value of the whole Bible.* The Hebrew Scriptures are the Word of God and have validity in and of themselves.

2. *Stress the profound Jewishness of Jesus and His teaching.* It is this that gives the Hebrew Bible its basic relevance for the Christian: that Jesus and the early Church accepted it as the Word of God for them and that Jesus' message *presumes* in his hearers people imbued with the divine message of *Torah.*

3. *Develop the ability to use Jewish sources.* Helpful use can be made of Talmud, targum, later commentators such as Rashi, etc. in proclaiming the meaning of the Hebrew Scriptures and the Apostolic Writings for today. There is a treasure of fresh insight into Jewish tradition which can provide often startling new insights for the Christian.

4. *Avoid dichotomizing* or making the parts of the Bible antithetical to each other. There is a rich plurality of vision in *each* of the Testaments. The relationship between Jews and Christians is properly one of dialogue rather than disputation, as is the relationship between the Testaments themselves.

To these four "rubrics" may be added the following two from the 1974 Vatican Guidelines:

5. *"The existing links between the Christian liturgy and the Jewish liturgy* will be born in mind. The idea of a living community in the service of God, and in the service of men for the love of God, such as it is realized in the liturgy, is just as characteristic of the Jewish liturgy as it is of the Christian one. To improve Jewish-Christian relations, it is important to take cognizance of those common elements of the liturgical life

(formulas, feasts, rites, etc.), in which the Bible holds an essential place.''

6. ''When commenting on biblical texts, emphasis will be laid on *the continuity of our faith with that of the earlier covenant*, in the perspective of the promises, without minimizing those elements of Christianity which are original. We believe that those promises were fulfilled with the first coming of Christ. But it is none the less true that *we still await their perfect fulfillment* in his glorious return at the end of time.'' (italics added).

The last admonition deserves some comment, for the understanding of promise / fulfillment touches on the deepest mysteries of our Faith and will, thus, never, perhaps, be finally and definitely articulated. The question also represents a sensitive and as yet not wholly resolved agenda item of the dialogue between Jews and Christians. In one sense Christians must, with the witness of the New Testament, always affirm the universal significance of the Christ-event for human history. In another (primarily eschatological rather than Christological) sense we must listen to the Jewish witness to the incomplete ''redeemedness'' of this world. Jews have maintained, in response to Christian claims, that for them the Messiah cannot be said to have come until the Messianic Age (''perfect fulfillment'') has been made manifest. The Messianic Age, they believe, is promised to be one of universal justice and peace, a true reign of God. Biblical scholars likewise discern a tension in the New Testament between the ''already here'' aspect of the fulfillment of the promises in Christ as Messiah an the ''not yet'' aspect of the awaited Kingdom, as well as the ''always here'' aspect of the eternal ''Kingdom within,'' a concept basic to Pharisaism and Jesus' teaching alike.

The above citation from the Vatican Guidelines, then, appears to call us to a renewed sense of humility in the articulation of our claims. With the Jews, we too await the ''perfect fulfillment'' of the promises. And within the mystery of election we too are called to witness to and to work for the upbuilding of God's Kingdom. From this perspective we can, in humility, admit today the possibility of a new, more positive understanding of our relationship with the Jewish people in God's overall plan for salvation. Though the precise nature of that relationship yet eludes our ability to articulate theologically, we do know that it is a hope-filled, positive one in which our own self-understanding is only diminished when framed in negative terminology toward the Jewish people.

A few practical suggestions will conclude this section:

1. Celebrating the Passover Seder

While it is recommended that candidates be urged to attend Jewish liturgical services, for spiritual as well as educational enrichment, the Bishops' Committee on the Liturgy has issued the following guidelines regarding the practice of "Christian" seders:

For many years it has been the custom of some Christians to celebrate the Passover seder during Holy Week. The Celebration of Passover is a sacred memorial, enjoined upon all Jews by the Scriptures and by post-biblical tradition. The Passover forms an integral part of Jewish family piety as well. (See "Passover," *Encyclopedia Judaica*, Vol. 13, 163-173.)

Thus when Christians celebrate this sacred feast among themselves the rites of the *haggadah* for the seder should be respected in all their integrity. The seder, whether celebrated in the home or as part of a parish's observance of the paschal mysteries, should be celebrated in a dignified manner and with sensitivity to those to whom the seder truly belongs. The primary reason why Christians may celebrate the festival of Passover should be to acknowledge common roots in the history of salvation. Any sense of "re-staging" the Last Supper of the Lord Jesus should be avoided, not only because biblical scholarship is not in accord as to the nature of that supper, but especially because it is the character of both Jewish and Christian liturgy to celebrate the events of salvation as an anamnesis memorial. The rites of the Triduum are the annual memorial of the events of Jesus' dying and rising.

The Liturgy Secretariat would recommend to groups and parishes only those editions of the haggadah which are true to the tradition of Israel and the authentic meaning of the festival of Passover. One such edition has been edited by Rabbi Leon Klenicki, with an introduction by Gabe Huck: *The Passover Celebration: A Haggadah for the Seder*. Copies of the booklet may be ordered from the Liturgy Training Program, Archdiocese of Chicago, 155 East Superior Street, Chicago, IL 60611 (312/751-8382). Single copy: $1.90; 10-99 copies: $1.50 each; 100 or more: $1.00 each.

2. Memorializing the Victims of the Holocaust

Yom HaShoah services memorializing the victims of the Holocaust can, if properly prepared and celebrated, provide occasions for increasing the sensitivity of candidates for the priesthood concerning Jews and Judaism. The National Conference of Christians and Jews (43 W. 57th Street, New York, NY 10019) has developed some excellent materials, including sample services and sermons, that can be easily adapted to the seminary as well as the parish setting.

3. Holy Week

Finally, the tensions and even violence toward the Jews that has erupted in many places in the past over the reading of the Passion narratives during Holy Week warn us that creative approaches are warranted today to avoid the misunderstandings that can occur during this intensely emotional period. Special programs during Lent on the background and significance of these texts, as well as on the history of antisemitism, need to be implemented to prepare students for their role in leading and interpreting the Holy Week liturgy. G. Sloyan's *Commentary on the New Lectionary* (Paulist, 1975) is excellent on the Sunday readings for Lent. As an example of what can be done on the local level, the Archdiocese of Los Angeles has issued "Lenten Pastoral Readings" to assist pastors and commentators throughout the Lenten season (available in the Archdiocesan "Guidelines for Ecumenical and Interreligious Relations," 1982).

Finally, two recent collections of essays, both the result of a collaborative, Catholic-Jewish editing, offer models for joint studies in liturgies: J. Petuchowski and M. Brocke gather a number of insightful essays in *The Lord's Prayer and Jewish Liturgy* (Seabury, 1978). And the results of an official dialogue sponsored by the Synagogue Council of America and the National Conference of Catholic Bishops are found in E. Fisher and D. Polish, eds., *Liturgical Foundations of Social Policy in the Catholic and Jewish Traditions* (University of Notre Dame Press, 1982).

C. CHURCH HISTORY

While dwelling on past misdeeds is never the most pleasant of exercises and should not be overdone, Catholics today, in the burning light of the fires of Auschwitz, truly need to come to grips with the history of Christian antisemitism. The value is both for the dialogue and for the sake of the Church itself.

On the level of dialogue Christians all too often seem to suffer from a sort of selective amnesia in which the unsavory elements of our history are forgotten. Yet anyone wishing to dialogue with Jews must be aware that a tragic past has shaped our present. That past must be acknowledged in order to be overcome for the sake of the future. The venomous antisemitism of the Patristic period, the sadistic violence of the Crusades and the Inquisition, the mass expulsions and pogroms that took place throughout "Christendom" with sickening regularity, need to be faced with honesty and candor.

But the other, positive side of the historical coin needs also to be stressed, perhaps especially so today. The Vatican Guidelines, in arguing that Catholic-Jewish relations should receive a high priority "even in areas where no Jewish communities exist," point out that these relations "concern the Church as such, since it is when pondering her own mystery that (the Church) encounters the mystery of Israel."

What we study Jewish-Christian history for, then, is not self-flagellation, but self-discovery. How, given the wide range of views toward Judaism (many positive) to be found in the New Testament, did we end up with a Marcion in the Second Century and with a full-blown "teaching of contempt" by the fifth? While Rosemary Reuther may be wrong in her assertion that anti-Judaism is inevitably the "left hand of Christology" *(Faith and Fratricide,* Seabury, 1974), her presentation of the antisemitic stance of a distressingly high percentage of the Church Fathers is material with which Christians need to become more familiar (see also D. Efroymson, "The Patristic Connection," A. T. Davies, *cit.,* 98-117).

Given this negative teaching toward Judaism, which became increasingly embedded in the Church legislation and Christian culture itself, it remains a challenge for Church historians to determine the extent to which the Christian teaching of contempt may have contributed to laying the groundwork for the Holocaust. Certainly there is no direct link between traditional Christian antipathy to Judaism and the Nazi policy of annihilation. Nazism, though it may have gained the support of many individual Christians, was fundamentally anti-Christian and the Nazi regime murdered millions of Catholics and Protestants, and thousands of priests and ministers throughout Europe. As the Jewish scholar, Y. Yerushalmi maintained in his essay in *Auschwitz: Beginning of a New Era?* (E. Fleishner, ed., KTAV, 1977), if Christian theology held within itself the seeds of genocide, these would have been acted upon at some point during the long course of the Church's political ascendancy in the Middle Ages. But they were not. Antisemitism existed in the world before the rise of Christianity and exists in the so-called "secular" culture today.

Yet the fact cannot be avoided that Christian theological, liturgical and canonical denigration of Judaism did help to make the Jews "marginal" in Western culture and, therefore, all too vulnerable to the power of Hitler's maniacal race-hatred. For American students, however, the question is not so much one of guilt for the past as of responsibility for the future. Christians need to understand the dynamics of prejudice, particularly in its most ancient and virulent form, antisemitism, in order to eradicate its many subtle manifestations from our society.

On the positive side, the heritage we have received from Judaism is not limited to the Hebrew Scriptures. Christianity and Judaism, through the ages, have continually interacted and cross-fertilized each other. There are Jewish modalities embedded in our music and our liturgy. Much of our doctrinal structure is rooted in Jewish thought. Many of the seeds of scholastic philosophy and of the Renaissance, for example, were brought to us by Jews whose contacts in the Muslim world enabled them to transfer developments from there into the Christian world.

Church history, the understanding of the development of the Catholic tradition, is impoverished if it is not at the same time Jewish history. The bibliography at the end of this booklet gives many resources for delving more deeply into the spiritual treasures of our common history.

D. CATECHETICS

1. Educational Principles

Basic to the catechetical enterprise, in terms of proper Jewish-Christian understandings, is the realization that catechetical formation does not exist in a vacuum. Rather, it must constantly seek to overcome the pervasive and subtle antisemitic tendencies which exist in American culture today. Neither educators nor students are free of this influence. A quick check of Webster's dictionary, for example, finds the word "Jewry" defined as "a ghetto" and "Pharisaical" as "hypocritical." Shakespeare's Shylock and Dickens' Fagin perpetuate stereotypes in literature. Even today, Jews are set apart as somehow "different" and, therefore, "dangerous." Antisemitism is one of the oldest known forms of racism and its tendrils are intertwined with our culture, attitudes, and even thought patterns.

Secondly, the study of Judaism in a Christian context cannot be merely a dispensing of information about a topic. It is a matter faith, for which the traditionally "objective" approach employed in comparative religion courses is not adequate.

For those training for the priesthood or other ministries, the encounter with Judaism is radically different—and potentially more enriching—than the study of any other world religion. The Talmud, as a record of the Jewish people living out the Sinai covenant in history, can be a document of more than historic interest. As people engrafted unto that covenant in Jesus, the Jew, (cf. Romans 9-11), it can address us directly in dialogue today.

2. Catechetical Strategy

Textbook studies of Catholic teaching materials, initiated in the late 1950's by the American Jewish Committee and recently updated (see bibliography) have shown the tremendous improvement that has taken place in Catholic catechetical treament of Jews and Judaism. Whereas before the Second Vatican Council Jesus was seldom seen as truly Jewish, today such statements are common. And the general approach to Judaism is both positive and well researched.

The inaccuracies that remain in Catholic textbooks tend to cluster in the treatment of New Testament themes, such as the portrayal of the Pharisees and in accounts of Jesus' passion and death. Ambiguous too (because the theology is still being developed) are statements dealing with the covenant relationship between Judaism and Christianity. As the 1974 Vatican Guidelines have their effect, and as the insights of contemporary biblical scholarship are integrated into the texts, it is to be hoped that the remaining vestiges of the teaching of contempt will disappear as they have already in their more blatant forms.

Catechetics has a significant role to play in the preparation of Catholics for hearing the Word proclaimed in the liturgy. The Scriptural and liturgical sections of this handbook, then, should be of assistance in structuring our catechesis to fulfill that role.

Finally, it should be noted that there is much in Jewish tradition that can be of benefit to Christian religious educators. The Seder, for example, is a liturgical rite that does catechesis of children quite naturally and beautifully within the family setting. Here again is an area where Christian life can be enriched by contact with living Judaism. (cf. E. Fisher, "The Family in Catholic and Jewish Traditions," *SIDIC* Vol. 14., no. 2, 1982, 4-15).

E. SYSTEMATICS

Recent works by Christians such as Marcel Dubois, Clemens Thoma, Paul van Buren, Alice and Roy Eckardt, Eva Fleischner, Edward Flannery, Andre LaCocque, Franklin Littlell, Monika Hellwig, Franz Mussner and Cornelius Rijk have joined an earlier generation of Christian scholars such as Jacques Maritain, Augustin Cardinal Bea, Charles Cardinal Journet, Jean Danielou, John Oesterreicher, Paul Tillich, James Parkes and Reinhold Niebuhr in grappling with the profound implications for Christian doctrine of the renewed attitude toward Judaism. While it is much too soon to assess the strengths and weaknesses of this theological outpouring, it is fair to say that almost every area of traditional systematic and moral theology will be touched, and enlivened, by its vision of hope and spiritual renewal. Many of these approaches are conveniently summarized in J. Pawlikowski, *What Are They Saying About Christian-Jewish Relations?* (Paulist, 1980).

Central to the theological enterprise is the sensitive question of how to articulate the covenant relationship. What does it mean to be in covenant, to be elect? Does Christian theology need to denigrate the Jewish covenant in order to affirm its own self-identity? What, precisely, does it mean to say that Judaism was not "abrogated" but "fulfilled" in the coming of Christ? What do we mean by "peoplehood?" What do Jews mean by it? These are but a few of the challenging questions posed in the dialogue between the Church and the Jewish people today.

Michael McGary, in *Christology After Auschwitz* (Paulist, 1977) handily surveys proposed solutions to the dilemmas of anti-Judaic Christian doctrinal formulations, including the debate over the question of only one covenant or two distinct covenants (pp. 72-97). More recently, Catholic scholars such as Monika Hellwig ("From the Jesus of Story to the Christ of Dogma" in A. T. Davies, ed., *Antisemitism and the Foundations of Christology*, (Paulist, 1979, 118-136), Gregory Baum ("Catholic Dogma After Auschwitz," *ibid.*, 137-150), Rosemary Radford Reuther ("Christology and Jewish-Christian Relations," A. J. Peck, ed., *Jews and Christians After Auschwitz*, Fortress, 1982, 22-38), and David Tracy ("Religious Values After the Holocaust: A Catholic View," *ibid.*, 87-107) have, in trenchant essays, begun to open up significant new areas in which there is need, in Hellwig's words, "for a reexamination of traditional syntheses of the Christian message." Clemens Thoma's *A Christian Theology of Judaism* (Paulist, 1980) also offers a number of provocative hints in this direction.

These writers note that the *Shoah* (the Holocaust) and the rebirth of a Jewish state in Eretz Israel, the one reaching "impossible" depths of human evil and the other conventionally considered a theological "impossibility" burst in on complacent systematic assumptions about both the nature of humanity and the nature of the divine-human relationship. Hellwig centers on soteriology, on the unquestioned assumptions embedded in Chalcedonian and later interpretations of the meaning of salvation, of grace and nature, salvation history and human history. Baum seeks to develop the "principles of doctrinal change" and the types of theological options available to those who would attempt to "de-ideologize" Christian tradition through reinterpretation rather than radical negation. Baum classifies Reuther among the "negators" *(cit.*, 150) with some justification though her latest summary of her thought (cf. above) contains constructive insights, as well as a very helpful critique of "three basic theological patterns that promote anti-Judaism," along with attempted "critical reconstructions of these theses." *(cit.*, 27) For Reuther, the central question remains Christological. The three "dualistic patterns" she takes up are: "the schism of judgment and premise" (28-32), "the schism of particularism and universalism" (32-33), and "the schisms of law/grace and letter/spirit (34-36).

The biblical, liturgical and even missiological developments of the last few decades raise fundamental questions for every area of theology, the implications of which are only now beginning to be tackled by our major systematicians. David Tracy, in his essay in *Jews and Christians After the Holocaust* (Fortress, 1982) notes that the Holocaust can fittingly be named "theologically the *tremendum* of our age." It raises anew not only the problem of theodicy, but even more so the question of anthropodicy, which is to say the adequacy of our traditional theological anthropology and of the theology of suffering. For Tracy, the realization that "there is no other God for the Christian than the God of Israel," and that Christology itself must "reaffirm on inner-Christian grounds the status of the Jews as God's chosen, covenanted people" means that re-formulations of key Christological themes will have to be undertaken by systematic theology today:

To employ the language of a proleptic Christology seems to me an appropriate route to take. For to affirm the belief in Jesus Christ is, for the Christian, to affirm the faith that in the ministry, death and resurrection of Jesus the decisive token, manifestation, prolepsis of the future reign of God (and thereby of Messianic times) is both already here in proleptic form (indeed, for myself has been manifested as always already here) and, just as really, not yet here (p. 100).

Such an "always / already / not yet" structure of the faith shatters many of the traditional dichotomies (promise / fulfillment, law / grace, etc.) on which so much of Christian systematic theology is built. New structures, such as those hinted at in the works of Tracy, Hellwig and others, will have to be built within the context of traditional faith, yet with a critical eye toward historically-conditioned expressions of that faith. A helpful analysis of major contemporary systematic theological schools, from continental thinkers (Pannenberg, Moltmann, Kung and Schillebeck) to the Latin American "liberation theologies" of Gutierrez, Bonino, Sobrino and Boff, with this need in mind, is provided in John T. Pawlikowski's *Christ in the Light of the Christian-Jewish Dialogue*(Paulist, 1982). Pawlikowski shows the weaknesses, and some surprising strengths, in these thinkers and goes on to suggest his own, tentative Christology. This effort too has its weaknesses, as he himself candidly admits. But it represents a beginning. It is to be hoped that other major Catholic thinkers will pick up where he left off. The misunderstandings of Jews and Judaism that pervade current Christian theology are, as this booklet has tried to illustrate, intertwined throughout our thinking. So there is a real urgency, and immensely hopeful potential, in taking up the challenge.

A good example of the range of issues raised in dialogue today can be found in the special issue of *The Journal of Ecumenical Studies*: "A Jewish-Christian Dialogue between Americans and Germans" (Winter, 1981). On the difficult question of mission and conversion, M. Cohen and H. Croner have edited a series of provocative essays for the Stimulus volume *Christian Mission / Jewish Mission* (Paulist, 1983).

For Paul van Buren, an Episcopal priest, *Discerning the Way* (Seabury, 1980) means a re-working of the structure of Christian doctrine from the ground up, since any adequate "theology of the Jewish-Christian reality" should enlighten the very roots of our faith. Others have noted the fundamental questions that arise in such diverse areas as ecclesiology (peoplehood / election / mission), eschatology (kingdom, the parousia delayed), and Christian anthropology (what does the Holocaust say about the nature of humanity, redemption and of evil itself?). The development of van Buren's major four-volume study of these questions, should provide continuing stimulus to Catholic as well as Protestant thought.

F. MORAL THEOLOGY

In moral theology, the Holocaust raises the question of theodicy in a dramatic, unique fashion which will be deeply challenging to students. Can one believe in a God who allowed such unprecedented evil? On a different level, the question is raised concerning the human capacity for evil: can one believe in our own Western "civilization" which perpetrated it? Is a rational moral system possible today in the face of such absolute irrationality? Such "hard questions" can transform an academic session into a serious spiritual struggle. The disturbing questions raised within Judaism by such thinkers as Elie Wiesel, Emil Fackenheim and Eliezer Berkovitz can challenge Christian theological responses just as they do Jewish.

Moral and social issues also provide an excellent opportunity for a dialogically-oriented approach in the classroom. The Christian social vision owes its origin to the divine call for justice and love embodied in the Torah and the prophets. Through the ages, the Jewish moral passion has witnessed to the true significance of God's kingdom. Much can be learned in these areas from Jewish literature on the subject.

Exciting dialogues are now taking place on all levels between our two communities. Nationally, the papers of two such meetings have been edited by E. Fisher and D. Polish as *Formation of Social Policy in the Catholic and Jewish Traditions* (University of Notre Dame Press), and *Liturgical Foundation of Social Policy in the Catholic and Jewish Traditions* (University of Notre Dame, 1982). Locally, the Archdiocese of Los Angeles, together with the American Jewish Committee and the Board of Rabbis have worked out joint statements on such difficult topics as "Abortion," "Caring for the Dying Person," "Kingdom," and "Covenant or Covenants?" The journal *SIDIC* has recently devoted several special issues to the joint Christian-Jewish exploration of such themes as "Man in the Perspective of the Kingdom" (Creation, Society, God), "The Chosen People," and "Jesus the Jew" (which reveals some of the amazingly positive views of Jesus coming out of the Jewish community today, especially in Israel). From the Jewish side as well, the book *Issues in the Jewish-Christian Dialogue: Jewish Perspectives on Covenant, Mission and Witness* (H. Croner and L. Klenicki, eds., Paulist-Stimulus, 1979) collects several important essays on topics of great concern to Christians.

From the Catholic side, the Central Committee of Roman Catholics in Germany has excellently summarized many of the "Basic Theological Issues of the Jewish-Christian Dialogue" *(Origins, November 22, 1979).* And the important "Study Outline on the Mission and Witness of the Church" prepared by Tommaso Federici for the 1977 meeting between the Vatican's Commission for Religious Relations with the Jews and the International Jewish Committee for Interreligious Consultations (IJCIC) raises critical issues that deserve further study (SIDIC, Vol. 11:13, 1978. 25-34), especially among missiologists.

The topic of the modern state of Israel will remain for some time a key issue raising theological as well as ethical concerns in the dialogue. While biblical fundamentalism and simplistic politicalization of the question should be avoided, Catholics do need to gain a deeper understanding of the relationship between Land and People within contemporary Judaism. The 1975 Statement of the American Bishops comments:

In dialogue with Christians, Jews have explained that they do not consider themselves as a church, a sect, or a denomination, as is the case among Christian communities, but rather as a peoplehood that is not solely racial, ethnic or religious, but in a sense a composite of all these. It is for such reasons that an overwhelming majority of Jews see themselves bound in one way or another to the land of Israel. Most Jews see this tie to the land as essential to their Jewishness. Whatever difficulties Christians may experience in sharing this view they should strive to understand this link between land and people which Jews have expressed in their writings and worship throughout two millenia as a longing for the homeland, holy Zion. Appreciation of this link is not given assent to any particular religious interpretation of this bond. Nor is this affirmation meant to deny the legitimate rights of other parties in the region, or to adopt any political stance in the controversies over the Middle East which lie beyond the purview of this statement.

Finally, it might be noted that, at the present stage, with the exception of Pawlikowski and a few others, it would seem to be Protestant rather than Catholic ethicians who are leading the way in seeking to draw out the ethical implications of the Holocaust for Christian reflection. One excellent recent example (stronger ethically than dogmatically from a Catholic point of view) is A. Roy and Alice Eckardt's passionate *Long*

Night's Journey into Day: Life and Faith after the Holocaust (Detroit: Wayne State University Press, 1982), which sees in the capacity of Christians to perpetrate the Holocaust an ethical critique of Christianity itself. A briefer, though also trenchant Protestant approach is to be found in T. R. Anderson's contribution to *Antisemitism and the Foundations of Christianity*: "An Ethical Critique: Antisemitism and the Shape of Christian Repentance," *(cit.*, 208-229). The extent to which Christian thought can be critiqued based on Christian (mis)deed, remains an outstanding one, and may depend on how one views the methodological relationship between theory and praxis, and, within theory, on the relationship between history and traditional doctrine.

That the event of the *Shoah* has had a lasting impression on moral thought in this century, however, is evidenced by the growing practice to apply the term *holocaust* to so many subsequent tragedies, from nuclear warfare and the Cambodian massacres to (somewhat less precisely) the wholesale practice of abortion on demand within contemporary American society. The appropriateness of the adoption of such categories by Christian moralists who may not always have taken the Holocaust deeply into their overall thinking on its implications for the Church's moral stance today is a question that would seem to call for some intensive self-scrutiny today.

Such ethical self-scrutiny in the wake of the Holocaust is becoming increasingly important in the field of Christian ethics today, as the works of Franklin Sherman and Franklin Littell have shown. The studies included in Littell and Locke, *The German Church Struggle and the Holocaust* (Wayne State University Press, 1974) provide more than simple historical reporting. At their heart, they are an ethical critique of recent history, a critique with deep implications for our understanding of the Church today (see F. H. Littell, "Ethics After Auschwitz," *Worldview*, September 1975, 22-26).

From a Catholic point of view, Gordon Zahn's *German Catholics and Hitler's Wars* and John F. Morley's *Vatican Diplomacy and the Jews During the Holocaust 1933-1943* (KTAV, 1980) are also written from a distinct, and distinctly critical moral viewpoint. From a purely objective, historiographical point of view, such works are open to the criticism of not paying sufficient attention to the efforts that *were* made (some more successful than others) by Christians to save Jewish lives. (cf. R. A. Graham, S.J., *Pius XII's Defense of Jews and Others, 1944-45* [Catholic League for Religious and Civil Rights, 1982]). Ironically, it might be noted here, a great deal of the evidence we have for such "deeds of righteousness" have been preserved for us by Jewish accounts and documents, such as those to be found in Yad va Shem in Israel. These stories are available in popular form in such works as P. Friedman, *Their Brothers' Keepers* (New York: Holocaust Library, 1978); F. Leboucher, *Incredible Mission* (Doubleday, 1969); A. Ramati, *The Assisi Underground: Priests Who Rescued Jews* (Stein and Day, 1978); and P. Hallie, *Lest Innocent Blood Be Shed* (Harper & Row, 1979) and can be particularly useful as hagiography and as a balancing (or at least "leavening") of the overall picture, though they do not blunt the cutting edge of the questions that Christians should raise about themselves.

From a Jewish point of view, Richard Rubenstein's *Power Struggle* (Scribner's Sons, 1974), *After Auschwitz* and *The Cunning of History* (Harper & Row, 1978), especially the latter, raise fundamental questions concerning the nature of power, the reality of the diabolical and the new, more radically evil forms of human society "pioneered" in the society-wide system (government bureaucracy plus big business) that underlay the massive social organization necessary for the running of the death camps. From a more specifically religious vantage, Rabbi Irving Greenberg's "Cloud of Smoke, Pillar of Fire: Judaism, Christianity and Modernity After the Holocaust," (in E. Fleischner, ed., *Auschwitz: Beginning of A New Era?*, KTAV / Cathedral Church of St. John the Divine / ADL, 1977) raises similarly trenchant points on what the "breaking of limits" embodied in Auschwitz does to previously accepted underpinnings of traditional morality. Greenberg's powerful conclusion, as he himself admits, raises a host of further challenges to Christian morality:

There has been a terrible misunderstanding of the symbol of the crucifixion. Surely, we understand now that the point of the account is the cry: 'My lord, my lord, why have you abandoned me?' Never again should anyone be exposed to such one-sided power on the side of evil—for in such extremes not only does evil triumph, but the Suffering Servant now breaks and betrays herself. Out of the Holocaust experience comes the demand for redistribution of power. The principle is simple. No one should ever have to depend again on anyone else's goodwill or respect for their basic security and right to exist. The Jews of Europe needed that goodwill and these good offices desperately—and the democracies and the church and the Communists and their fellow-Jews failed them. No one should ever be equipped with less power than is necessary to assure one's dignity. To argue dependence on law, or human goodness or universal equality is to join the ranks of those who would like to repeat the Holocaust. Anyone who wants to prevent a repetition must support a redistribution of power. Since this, in turn, raises a large number of issues and problems with regard to power, we will not analyze it here. But the analysis of the risks of power and the dialectic of its redistribution is a central ongoing task of religion and morality, and a vast pedagogical challenge to all who are committed to prevent a second Auschwitz.

G. CURRICULUM OUTLINE

The following outline provides a checklist of major topics which can profitably be integrated into appropriate courses, or form an elective course of its own. It will also serve to summarize major points raised in this handbook.

1. The Hebrew Scriptures (Tanakh, Torah)

a. Essentially valid in their own right as an integral revelation for the Jewish people that is not exhausted in typological reference.

b. The continuity of the Hebrew views of God and morality with those of the New Testament, e.g., the Law of Love (Deut. 6:5; Lev. 19:18). The role of prophets as proclaimers of God's Law rather than mere predicters of future events.

c. Rabbinic teaching (Oral Torah) as a sound application of biblical teaching to changing circumstances in Jewish history (The Babylonian Exile, the Destruction of the Temple in the year 70 of the Common Era, etc.)

2. Judaism in New Testament Times

a. Richness and diversity of religious movements in the period.

b. Pharisees as religious reformers, opposed to the fundamentalism of the Sadducees, the wealthy aristocracy of Herod, and those who collaborated with Roman Imperialism.

c. Jesus' teaching as essentially Jewish in tone and content (e.g., Luke 11:37; 13:31; Acts 5, 23).

3. The First Century Split

a. Jesus, Mary, and the Apostles as observant Jews.

b. Background of the split between Synagogue and the early Church; a family quarrel. How this split is reflected in the evolution of the present Gospel narratives.

c. St. Paul and the mission to the Gentiles. Romans 9-11 and a living relationship between the Covenants.

d. Overview of the various theological approaches to Judaism by New Testament authors, positive and negative, (e.g., Epistle to the Hebrews) within the context of the New Testament as a whole, and of developments within the Jewish community of the time.

e. A careful use of the historical-critical approach to the Passion Narratives and of Church Tradition (Trent, Vatican II) on the question of responsibility.

f. Background for the attacks on the Pharisees in Matthew, and John's theological use of the term, "the Jews."

4. Rabbinic and Medieval Judaism

a. The rise of the Synagogue; the thought of leading figures in the movement (Hillel, Akiba); impact of the Synagogue on Christian thought and ritual.

b. The school of Jamnia and Rabbi Johanan ben Zakkai.

c. Talmud: Mishnah, Gemara, and Responsa.

d. Medievel Commentators: Rashi (11th c.), the Shulchan Aruch, Nachmanides, Ibn Ezra, the Kimchis, etc.)

e. Jewish Philosophy: Ibn Gabriol, Maimonides, Judah Ha-Levi, Saadia Gaon, etc.

f. Jewish life: Babylonian Jewry, the Golden Age in Spain, the Ghetto, the Crusades, expulsion and forced conversion.

g. Jewish liturgy: the festivals and the Sabbath.

h. Jewish views of Christianity (Maimonides, Jacob Emden, Ha-Levi, Meiri, etc.). The Disputations and Church legislation on the Jews.

5. Reformation to 20th Century

a. The Inquisition and the Auto da Fe.

b. Martin Luther and antisemitism.

c. The Enlightenment: Spinoza, Mendelssohn, etc.

d. Hasidism and Jewish Mysticism.

e. Philosophy and Literature: Heinrich Heine, Martin Buber, Franz Rosenzweig, etc.

f. Eastern Europe: the Shtetl culture; the Jewish community of Poland as the intellectual and spiritual heart of world Jewry.

6. Judaism in an Age of Pluralism

a. Emancipation and Assimilation.

b. Reform, Conservative, and Orthodox Judaism.

c. the American Jewish Community: religious and communal organizations, immigration, contributions to American history, Jewish richness and diversity.

7. Nazi Genocide (Endlosung, Shoah)

a. The role of theological anti-Judaism and the silence of the Churches, along with a mature appreciation of what the Churches *did* accomplish within the limited means at their disposal. This represents a complex and still unresolved set of historical and moral questions.

b. Hitler and neo-pagan nationalism.

    c. The death camps and the destruction of East European Jewry.

    d. Christian and Jewish resistance: "The Righteous among the Nations," Franz Jagerstatter, Dietrich Bonhoeffer, Warsaw Ghetto Uprising, Raoul Wallenberg, etc.

    e. Holocaust Literature: Anne Frank, Elie Wiesel, Victor Frankl. Holocaust Theology: E. Fackenheim, I. Greenberg, E. Berkovits, F. Littell, P. van Buren, A. & R. Eckardt, A. Davies, F. Sherman, M. Barth, H. J. Cargas, etc.

    f. Catholic theology in the light of the Holocaust: M. Dubois, J. Maritain, J. Pawlikowski, C. Thoma, F. Mussner, E. Fleischner, M. Hellwig, C. Rijk, G. Baum, R. Reuther, J. Oesterreicher, D. Tracy, H. Kung, L. Swidler, etc.

8. Zionism and the Modern State of Israel

    a. Early Zionism: Theodore Herzl and Ahad Haam.

    b. The British Mandate and the Balfour Declaration.

    c. The meaning of the rebirth of Israel for the American Jewish community. Early Christian reactions to the establishment of the State.

    d. Its meaning for Christian-Jewish relations today.

III. Spiritual Formation

he spiritual tradition of Judaism is immensely rich and varied. Unfortunately, it is all but unknown to Christians, save for the more recent works of Martin Buber, Elie Wiesel and Abraham Joshua Heschel.

Jewish spirituality is, in its essence, coexistive with Jewish life. It manifests itself in prayer, liturgy, the approach to study of Torah, and even in ethics as a form of piety. Many of the great Jewish mystics, for example, were also scholars of *halachah* (Jewish law). A good overview, written by Catholics, can be found in *The Spirituality of Judaism* by R. LeDeaut, A. Jaubert, and K. Hruby (Abbey Press, Religious Experience Series, Vol. 11, 1977).

Of great interest to Catholics will be the medieval *piyyut* or liturgical prayer tradition, which flows with a sense of the intimacy of God as a living presence. Indeed, the Hebrew term for union with God in mystical literature is *devekut*, the word Genesis uses when Adam is commanded to "cleave unto his wife." Ibn Gabriol's poetry (see I. Zanqwill, transl., *Selected Religious Poems*, JPS 1923) and his masterpiece, *The Kingly Crown* (B. Lewis, transl., London: Vallentine, Mitchell, 1961) are spiritual classics which Christians can share.

One area of particularly profitable meditation and study lies in the Jewish tradition of ethical piety. Max Kadushin's *Worship and Ethics* (Northwestern Ed., 1964) provides a systematic digest of halakhic practices touching on prayer and ethics. Bahya ibn Pakuda's 11th century masterpiece *Duties of the Heart* (M. Hyamson, Bloch, 1962) is a work with many resonances for the Catholic. Moses Hayim Luzatto (1707-1746) wrote classic texts in both ethics *(The Path of the Upright,* transl. by M. Kaplan for JPS, 1966) and mysticism *(General Principles of the Kabbalah,* S. Weiser, 1970).

Kabbalah, which means "tradition," represents a vast literature of esoteric mysticism. Its *magnum opus,* the *Sefer ha Zohar* (Book of Splendor) runs to many volumes and has its roots in the mystical trends of the early centuries of the Common Era. Rich in symbolism and multiple layers of meaning, it needs a good introduction to be understandable to the Christian. Perhaps the best is *Gerschom Scholem's Major Trends in Jewish Mysticism* (Schocken, 1961).

A movement deeply influenced by the *Kabbalah* but which developed on a popular level is that of *Hasidism.* The medieval forerunner of this movement can be found in Judah ben Samuel's 13th century work, *Sefer Hasidim* (Book of the Pious), which combines the practice of communal charity with individual asceticism and the pursuit of Communion of God *(devekut).* Its later form, perhaps best known to us through the works of Martin Buber *(Hasidism and Modern Man* and *The Origin and Meaning of Hasidism,* both translated by M. Friedman for Harper and Row) originated in Eastern Europe in the 18th century. Hasidism provided a rich spiritual life and unique insights into prayer by sacralizing everyday realities and making every activity a form of prayer. Useful collections of Hasidic tales can be found in J. Mintz, *Legends of the Hasidim* (University of Chicago, 1968) and L. Newman, *Hasidic Anthology* (Schocken, 1963). A more general collection of Jewish religious folktales in English can be found in volume two of M. J. Ben Gurion's *Mimekor Yisrael (Indiana University, 1976).*

One of the most important Jewish mystics is Abraham Isaac Kook (1865-1935), the first chief rabbi of Eretz Israel. Paulist Press' "The Classics of Western Spirituality" series includes an excellent translation of Kook's major writings by B. Z. Bokser (1978) as well as a collection of the classical Hasidic Tales of Nachman of Bratslav (1978).

The essential source of insight into Jewish spirituality, however, remains the liturgy itself, both in the synagogue and the home services. The Sabbath and the feasts define, as many commentators have noted, what it means to be a Jew in living (sometimes struggling, but always constant) intimacy with God. Handy general introductions can be found in W. Simpson, *Light and Rejoicing* (Belfast, 1976), S. Rosenberg, *Judaism* (Paulist, 1966), and B. Martin, *Prayer in Judaism* (Basic Books, 1968), as well as in the prayer books themselves and the works of Heschel. A recent collection of Jewish and Christian essays on prayer delve more deeply into individual aspects and commonalities as well as differences in prayer life: A. Finkel and L. Frizzell, *Standing Before God: Studies on Prayer in Scriptures and in Tradition* (KTAV, 1981).

Finally, Anglican pastor Alan Ecclestone reminds us in his study of Jewish-Christian relations that the *Shoah*, the Holocaust, can only be properly approached in a spirit of prayer, and that the event, which David Tracy has called, quite properly, "theologically the *tremendum* of our age" faces us with a truly profound spiritual challenge, a dark night of the soul:

It is therefore a major concern of the spiritual education of our time that we face the fact of Auschwitz. To Peter Cauchon's question in the epilogue to Shaw's *St. Joan*, 'Were not the sufferings of our Lord Christ enough for you?', we must for our generation answer No. Our meditations on the Passion were not sufficient to awaken us to the realities of a world in which antisemitism flourished. To set our faces in another direction we have to see ourselves as participants in it. We came on the scene after centuries of acquiescence in evil things had prepared us for this Final Operation...Their analysis is of supreme importance to the shaping of a relevant spirituality for your time. *(The Night Sky of the Lord*, Schocken, 1982, p. 17).

Ecclestone thus sees his study primarily as a book of meditations, a call to prayer, to the "profound change of heart" and opening of the eyes that constitutes, in biblical terminology, *teshuvah*, a turning back to the Lord. The Anglican pastor's language here is, independently, strikingly similar to that used by the Pope in his recent address on Jewish-Christian relations to representatives of bishops' conferences around the world. The Pope too spoke of the persecutions of the Jews as having finally "opened well many eyes" and "overturned (disturbed) many hearts." In view of our "common spiritual patrimony," a concept he specifically expands to include not only biblical but traditional and contemporary Jewish spirituality, the Pope concludes that "Christians are on the good road" in persevering in the task of renewal of Christian-Jewish relations.

This spiritual, inwardly transformative aspect of openness to "the stranger" is, of course, most deeply facilitated by the actual practice of dialogue. Silent meditation too, especially during Lent, can be enhanced by prayerful exposure to the photographic images of the events of the *Shoah*. H. J. Cargas' *A Christian Response to the Holocaust* (Stonehenge, 1981) in its central section brings together a number of graphic photographs, with brief meditative responses for each. "Where," he asks, "was Christ at Auschwitz?" (p. 137). Much less graphic (indeed, not a single overtly violent picture is included) are the photographs of *The Auschwitz Album* (Random House, 1980), based upon a collection of photos originally taken of the death camp be a nameless Nazi photographer. The album was discovered by Lili Meier, a survivor of the camp.

A simple, moving text has been added by Peter Hellman. Here, the horror is latent, and all the more powerful for its latency, as we follow groups of Hungarian Jews from their arrival at the Birkenau train platform to the doors of (but not within) the gas chambers themselves. What, we wonder, did they know of the fate in store for them?

The term *Shoah*, by the way, is the Hebrew word for the Holocaust. It is a biblical, prophetic term, indicating a searing, dessicating wind that scours the earth of all life. It is the antithesis of the biblical *ruah*, God's creative breath / wind (Gn. 1:2), the Spirit. It is radically, uncreation. Chaos.

IV. Field Education

bviously, the best form of field experience for inter-religious understanding is active involvement in a Christian-Jewish dialogue. The diocesan ecumenical officer will be able to work with the field director to establish how best students might be able to fit into existing programs or help to set up new ones geared to their needs as well as the community's.

Dialogue does not occur only on the official, diocesan level. Many parishes located near synagogues have active programs, ranging from pulpit exchanges to regular meetings to formal programs open to the public. The experience of participating in, or even initiating such programs, can be invaluable.

Likewise, if there is a Jewish seminary or *Yeshivah* nearby, the students, with faculty assistance, could develop an intensive, ongoing dialogue group of their own, which could then begin to tackle many of the more sensitive, and theological, issues being discussed on the national and international levels. One university, Temple University, has had an intriguing program which involves their own students doing research on particular areas of Christian-Jewish concerns and then sharing the results with theology students in several German universities working on the same areas.

In most sections of the country, there are field offices of the major Jewish organizations such as the American Jewish Committee. These are staffed by professionals and are active in a wide range of community and interreligious issues. The director of field experiences can contact these representatives and together work out programs for placing students in activities which would help them develop both their pastoral and their social skills.

In such activities as working together with the Jewish community for common social goals, it is always advisable that the dialogical and reflective elements of the experience not be forgotten. Students should be encouraged to sit down with their Jewish co-workers to share the meaning of their joint actions for each of them on a religious level. What is the motivation for and the goal of their respective communities' intense involvement in ameliorating the social conditions of society? What, in our respective religious traditions, forms the foundation for social involvement? How does it relate to essential faith questions, such as the yearning to help build the Kingdom of God on earth? Both the Jewish and the Catholic communities in America have been significant in creating organizations to foster social justice, in the building of hospitals, in the labor and civil rights movement, and in founding educational enterprises of all varieties. How, in realistic terms, can such commonly motivated activities help to establish a sense of shared witness between Church and synagogue for the sake of proclaiming the Name of the One God in today's world? What is the significance of joint social programming between Catholics and Jews for the longer range dialogue now occurring between us?

If the students are encouraged to debrief their experience with Jews in such terms, they will not only undergo training in specific pastoral skills but also, it is to be hoped, emerge with a clearer sense of the nature of the Church's mission in and for the world. Reflecting jointly in the implications of their attempts to embody the prophetic vision in reality together with Jews, who are passionately committed to the same vision, cannot help but deepen their own understanding of what it means to be a Christian.

V. Presenting Jews and Judaism in Theological Education

A. THE 1985 VATICAN "NOTES"

n the feast of Jewish saint, John the Baptist, June 24, 1985, the Holy See issued *Notes on the Correct Way to Present Jews and Judaism in Preaching and Catechism* (USCC Publ. no. 970). The document has significant implications for all of the categories discussed so far, and it opens up challenging new areas of reflection as well.

In this country, the 1985 *Notes* precipitated the development of three documents with a practical orientation to assist theological educators in their implementation of the *Notes*. These are: *Within Context, Guidelines for the Catechetical Presentation of Jews and Judaism in the New Testament* (Silver Burdett and Ginn, 1987), *Criteria for the Evaluation of Depictions of the Passion* (Bishops' Committee for Ecumenical and Interreligious Affairs, 1988), and *God's Mercy Endures Forever: Guidelines for Homilists* (Bishops' Committee on the Liturgy, in process). Together with the *Notes*, these documents greatly increase the specific tools available to Catholic theological education today.

In its first section, "Religious Teaching and Judaism," the *Notes* reaffirm that the "concern for Judaism in Catholic teaching is "not merely historical or archeological." Rather, founded on the design of the God of the Covenant," it occupies an "essential" place that needs to be "organically integrated" into Church teaching on all levels in order to develop "due awareness of the faith and religious life of the Jewish people as they are professed and practiced still today".

This continuing relevance for Catholic teaching of the history of Israel *after* the New Testament period and of Jewish religious thought throughout the centuries to the present is emphasized in various ways throughout the *Notes*. It constitutes a remarkable advance in the Church's reflection on the implications of *Nostra Aetate* and a remarkable challenge to the way in which Christians are called to "do theology" today.

In its section on the relationship between the Hebrew and Christian Scriptures (terminology not yet used by the *Notes* but used by the Pope increasingly in more recent years), for example, it urges Christians to "profit discerningly from the traditions of Jewish reading" of Sacred Scripture. This clearly implies some introduction to rabbinics and contemporary Jewish biblical scholarship for those training for the priesthood and the diaconate, whose role will be to interpret Scripture to the community during the liturgy.

The *Notes* likewise see "the pre-emanence of Israel, while so many ancient peoples have disappeared without trace," as "a sign to be interpreted within God's design" (Section VI). Thus, while cautioning against adopting at this early stage of dialogue "any particular religious interpretation" of major events in the history of the people of Israel since the time of Christ, it does see ongoing Jewish history as having very real theological relevance for the Church's own understanding of "God's design" for humanity, mentioning specifically the two great events of Jewish history of our time, the Holocaust (*Shoah*) and the rebirth of a Jewish state in the Land of Israel as suitable topics for careful theological reflection in Catholic seminaries and schools of theology.

Sections III–V of the *Notes*, as we have done above, seek to draw out the positive aspects of the Jewish roots of Christian teaching and liturgical practice, and within this positive frame to deal with the more negative portraits in the New Testament of Jesus' relationships with his people (see Chapter II, section A, 2, above).

Regarding the former, the *Notes* stress that Jesus is to be presented as "fully a man of his time and of his environment," a Jew of the Second Temple period. Jesus shared "the anxieties and hopes" of his people, and was "observant of the law," like any Jew of his time," though he showed "great liberty" and remarkable personal authority in his interpretation of Torah within the wide spectrum of Jewish interpretations that were characteristic of pre-rabbinic Judaism. Of all the wide variety of Jewish groups of the day, the *Notes* conclude, Jesus was perhaps closest to the Pharisees (precursors of the rabbis) in his attitudes and teachings. He shared with them distinctive doctrines, such as the resurrection of the body; forms of piety like alms-giving (*tsedakah*), fasting, and addressing God as Father in prayers; the use of parables in teaching; the formation of a "master-disciple" table fellowship

(*Havurah*) to observe Jewish feasts such as Passover; and the priority of the commandments to love God and neighbor. Paul, too, the *Notes* remind us, saw his own membership as a Pharisee "as a title of honor" (Acts 23:6-8, 26:5, Phil 3:5).

Many of the "controversies" depicted in the New Testament between Jesus and "the" Pharisees, then, had their original context in Jesus' participation in ongoing *internal* Pharisaic disputes, such as those regarding *divorce* (Mt. 5:31-32) where Jesus sides with and even goes beyond the more stringent Pharisaic House of Shammsi (Mishnah Gittin 90:1); plucking grain on the *Sabbath* (Mt 21), where he sides with (and typically goes beyond) the more lenient ruling of the House of Hillel (Shabbat 128 a; cf. Mekilta 31:13); and favoring a non-literal application of the general biblical principle of equivalency of punishment to the crime (Mt 6:38-42; cf. Ex. 21, Dt. 12, Lev. 24), the interpretation ultimately adopted by rabbinic Judaism (*Baba Kama* 8:1, 83b-84).

The *Notes* strongly affirm the hermeneutical principle introduced above (p. 42) that various New Testament "references hostile or less than favorable Jews have their historical context in conflicts between the nascent Church and the Jewish community" at the *end* of the first century when the gospels were set down, and that "certain controversies" depicted between Jesus and his fellow Jews "reflect Christian-Jewish relations long after the time of Jesus" (*Notes*, Section IV). Establishing the proper *historical context* of the gospel texts, thus, "is of capital importance" in theological education for preachers and catechists.

B. ST. PAUL AND THE LAW

Understanding the historical context, it may be added, is particularly important for understanding the letters of St. Paul, which were not written as a systematic theology, but as reactions to specific events or groups in the communities addressed. Chief among St. Paul's concerns, of course, is the argument over whether gentile converts needed first to become Jews (i.e. be Torah-observant) or whether acceptance of Christ was sufficient. As reflected in Acts 15, of course, this was the central issue of the first great "Council" of the Church, the Council of Jerusalem. Terrance Callan in *Forgetting the Root* (Paulist, 1986) uses this issue to distinguish among four main groups of Christians in the New Testament period: conservative Jewish and conservative Gentile Christians on the one hand, and liberal Jewish and liberal Gentile Christians on the other. Conservative Christians would answer, "yes," converts must adopt Judaism in order to become Christian. Liberal Christians argued, "no," they need not. Matthew, James, and perhaps the Gospel of John would be examples of the former approach, while Mark,

Luke-Acts and Paul would typify the latter. Matthew's gospel, for example, is almost unique in presenting a consistent replacement theology for the relationships between the covenants. But Matthew is equally insistent, as part of that same theology, that all Christians (gentile or Jewish), must observe the Law, indeed observe it more stringently than even the Pharisees (cf. also S. T. Lach, *A Rabbinic Commentary on the New Testament*, ICTAV/ADL 1987, for particularly rich Jewish insights on the Synoptic Gospels).

Many scholars today see the issues confronted by the Council of Jerusalem (Acts 15; related differently by Paul himself in Gal 2-4) as the key to interpreting Paul's essentially positive attitude toward the Law for Jews, while at the same time rejecting its application to Gentile converts to Christ.

In Christ, Paul argues, Gentiles can now become God's children (Gal. 4:21-31), a status previously reserved for Jews, who are already in convenant with God (Romans 9:4-5). In Christ, however, God's mercy is "manifested apart from the Law" (Rom. 3:21; 9:6-18) as well as through the Law (Rom. 2:18, 25). "Does God belong to the Jews alone?", Paul asks poignantly in Romans 3:29. "Is he not also the God of the Gentiles?" Paul's central vision is not an "either/or", as gentile Christians in later centuries were to frame it, but a "both/and." "Are we abolishing the law by means of faith? Not at all!", Paul thunders. "It is the same God who justifies the circumcized and the uncircumcized . . ." (Rom. 3:30-31). It is time, I believe, to take Paul's demurral seriously.

Many more texts need to be dealt with on this question than can here be considered. Philip Cunningham conveniently summarizes recent scholarly research on Paul in *Jewish Apostle to the Gentiles* (23rd Publ., 1986). L. Klenicki and E. Fisher present the larger issues in popular form in *Root and Branches: Biblical Judaism, Rabbinic Judaism and Early Christianity* (Winona, MN: St. Mary's Press, 1987, 24 pp).

C. NEW THEOLOGICAL QUESTIONS: THE JEWISH "NO," ESCHATOLOGY AND TYPOLOGY

The *Notes* do not skirt the hard issues, but confront them head on. While not fully answering all the questions they raise, they do help to clarify them for proper consideration within the context of theological education. This must be considered a major advance over previous documents.

The first is the so-called Jewish "no" for Jesus as a "Messiah". In what does this consist? It is, the *Notes* state, "a fact not merely of history but of theological bearing, of which St. Paul tries hard to plumb the meaning (Rom. 9-11)," and which, to some extent "remains a mystery hidden with God (Rom. 11:25)." These references (in Section IV of the *Notes*), which the *Notes* do not expand upon, are frankly tantalizing. Can we say, as St. Paul seems to hint (though in negative terms) in Romans 11:11 ("by their transgression salvation has come to the Gentiles") and in Romans 11:28 ("enemies of the gospel *for your sake*"), that the Jewish "No" to our Christological claims reflects in the same way God's will for the Jews, as well as for the Church? Put another way, do the Jewish people continue to have a divinely-willed vocation in and for the world of its own that was not exhausted in its earlier role (well performed) in preparing for Christ's *first* coming?

The structure and very clear assertions of the *Notes* would seem to argue for an affirmative Christian response to this question. Shortly after raising the above questions, the *Notes* do expand upon the earlier affirmation found in the 1974 *Guidelines* that "the history of Israel did not end in A.D. 70." To this, the *Notes* add: "it continued, especially in a numerous Diaspora which allowed Israel to carry to the whole world a witness—often heroic— of its fidelity to the one God and 'to exalt him in the presence of all the living' (Tbit 13:4)".

This statement is remarkable in several ways, not least of which is its implicit acknowledgement that the thousands of Jews who have died, over the centuries, at Christian hands for refusing to be forcibly converted to Christianity, thereby gave valid "heroic witness" (i.e. true martyrdom) to God in faithfulness to the divine covenant that is theirs. One might speculate, based upon this profound insight, that the Church may one day revise, for universal commemoration, the ancient feast of "the Holy Maccabees, Martyrs (August 1), and include in it also a commemoration of subsequent Jewish martyrs over the centuries, especially the victims of the Holocaust.

Indeed, one can see such a perspective developing, theologically if not liturgically, in recent teaching of Pope John II. On April 13, 1986, John Paul became the first Pope to visit and pray with Jews in a Synagogue since St. Peter. There, after listening appreciatively and affirmatively to a contemporary rabbinic interpretation of Genesis 17 (the covenant with Abraham, including the unconditional gift of the Land of Israel to the Jews), the Pope stated that "the Jewish religion is not extrinsic for us (the Church), but in a certain way is intrinsic to our own religion. With Judaism, therefore, we have a relationship which we do not have with any other religion . . . (We are) joint trustees and witnesses of an ethic marked by the Ten Commandments, in the observance of which humanity finds its truth and freedom." Acknowledging the real theological differences that divide Jews and Christians over the identity of the Messiah, and clearly rejecting all forms of syncretism between the two sister traditions, the Pope still projects a vision of a *shared* "trusteeship" in and joint witness to God's covenantal design for all humanity.

More recently, the Pope has added a specific, contemporary element to Christian understanding of the ongoing vocation of the Jewish people in God's design. Speaking to the tiny remnant of the once-magnificent Jewish community of Warsaw, the Pope stressed the uniqueness and priority of Jewish suffering during the Holocaust. The Jewish people's crucial witness to the *Shoah*, he said, constitutes a "saving warning" to all humanity, including the Church itself, revealing the "particular vocation" and "mission" of the Jews as "still the heirs of that election to which God is faithful." And, the *Notes* might add, the Jews are also faithful to God.

This statement acknowledges a specific, post-New Testament prophetic role for the Jewish people in God's saving design, a witness not exhausted even in that of the Hebrew Scriptures. John Paul's re-affirmation in Miami of the need for Christian education on all levels to concentrate efforts on a study of the historical events and theological implications of the *Shoah* takes on a profound urgency, since this is a task related to the very heart of the Church's own mission in and to the world.

In its most controversial section (II), the Vatican *Notes* tackle the issue of *typology*. While affirming Christian typological interpretation of the Hebrew Scriptures, especially as used in the liturgy (the Hebrew Scriptures themselves and not just the New Testament, after all, utilize typology as an interpretive device), the *Notes* seek to place our understanding of it within the larger, eschatological framework central to Jesus' teaching and therefore to the Church's proclamation.

Both Exodus/Sinai (the founding event of Judaism) and Incarnation/ Resurrection (upon which the Church is founded), are events of salvation history which are at once "already accomplished" and yet only "gradually realized". Both will, we pray (e.g. in the *Our Father*) make way for the fulfillment of God's design, which awaits its final consummation in ". . . the coming or return of the Messiah." The Jewish "no" in other words, may be a salvifically necessary reminder to the Church, as well as to the whole humanity, of the "not yet" aspect of redemption, a divinely willed good to Christians to "accept our responsibility to prepare the world of the coming of the Messiah by working together" *with* Jews and no longer *against* Jews for that day for which we so deeply long, the day when "the whole of creation will be transferred in Christ (Rom. 8:19-23)."

From this perspective, Cardinal Joseph Ratzinger has recently noted, the New Testament itself is to be seen as only "partial fulfillment" of the biblical promises. From the perspective of which we are all called by God, "Jews and Christians meet in a comparable hope, founded on the same promise" (Gn. 12:1-3, Heb. 6:13-18). While much remains "unresolved," this larger perspective is clear today and should permeate every area of Catholic theological education.

Resource Bibliography

A. DOCUMENTATION

"Basic Theological Issues of the Jewish-Christian Dialogue," Central Committee of Roman Catholics in Germany, May 8, 1979 *(Origins,* Vol. 9, 375-9).

"A Change in Attitude," Catholic Bishops of the Federal Republic of Germany, 1976.

"Declaration on Non-Christian Religions," The Second Vatican Council *(Nostra Aetate,* no. 4. October 28, 1965).

"Guidelines for Catholic-Jewish Relations," Secretariat for Catholic-Jewish Relations, National Conference of Catholic Bishops (NCCB), 1967.

"Guidelines and Suggestions for Implementing the Conciliar Declaration, *Nostra Aetate,*" Vatican Commission for Religious Relations with the Jews, December, 1974.

National Catechetical Directory, United States Catholic Conference (USCC), 1979, No. 77.

"Overcoming Difficulties," Remarks of Pope John Paul II *(Origins,* Vol. 8, 690 ff).

"Pastoral Orientations on the Attitude of Christians to Judaism," Episcopal Committee of the Roman Catholic Bishops of France, April, 1973.

"The World Council of Churches Ecumenical Considerations on Jewish-Christian Dialogue," Information and Documentation Bulletin of the International Council of Christians and Jews (Heppenheim, W. Germany, August 1982).

These and other documents, up to 1977, can be found in Helga Croner, ed., *Stepping Stones to Further Jewish-Christian Relations* (Stimulus / Anti-Defamation League of the B'nai B'rith, 1977), and in French, M-T. Hochet and B. Dupuy, *Les Eglises devant le Judaisme 1948-1978* (Paris: Cert, 1980).

Other statements of Pope John Paul II, such as his homily at Auschwitz and his address to the Jewish community of Mainz, can be found in J. Sheerin and J. Hotchkin, eds., *John Paul II: Addresses and Homilies on Ecumenism 1978-80* (USCC Publications, 1981).

Commentaries by Catholics on these documents can be found in E. Fisher, "The Vatican Guidelines: An Appraisal" *(Michigan Academician*, Vol. 9, 1976, 43-59), and

McGarry, C.S.P., Michael, *Christology After Auschwitz* (Paulist, 1977).

Mejia, J., "Survey of Issues" *(Origins*, Vol. 7, May 1978, 744-8).

Swidler, L., "Catholic Statements on Jews—A Revolution in Progress" *(Judaism*, Summer 1978, 299-307).

Many dioceses have developed their own guidelines for Catholic-Jewish Relations. J. B. Long has collected several excellent early articles in *Judaism and the Christian Seminary Curriculum* (Loyola University, 1966).

Finally, the journal *SIDIC* (via del Plebescito 112, 00186, Rome, Italy) has an English-language edition devoted exclusively to Christian-Jewish relations. Also in English, *Emmanuel* (P.O.B. 249, Jerusalem, Israel) presents the fruits of Christian-Jewish dialogue in Israel, biblical as well as theological. ADL's *Face to Face and AJC's Interreligious Bulletin* and *Christian-Jewish Relations: A Documentary Survey* are also helpful journals for the Seminary Library. For those who read German, the *Freiberger Rundbrief* is an annual review of significant developments in the field.

B. SACRED SCRIPTURE

Abrahams, I., *Studies in Pharisaism and Other Gospels* (N.Y.: KTAV, 1967).

Anderson, B., ed., *The Old Testament and Christian Faith* (Herder, 1969).

Barr, J. *Old and New Interpretation* (Harper and Row, 1966).

Boadt, L., Croner, H., and Klenicki, L. *Biblical Studies: Meeting Ground of Jews and Christians* (Paulist Stimulus, 1980).

Cohen, H. *The Trial and Death of Jesus* (KTAV, 1977).

Davies, A., ed. *Antisemitism and the Foundations of Christianity* (Paulist, 1979).

Fisher, E. *Faith Without Prejudice* (Paulist, 1977)

_____ "From Polemic to Objectivity: The Use and Abuse of Hebrew Sources in New Testament Scholarship," *Hebrew Studies Journal* (Nat'l Assoc. of Professors of Hebrew, Fall 1980, Vol. 20, 199-208).

_____ "Continuity and Discontinuity in the Scriptural Readings," *(Liturgy*, May 1978, 30-37).

Fiedler, P. *Jesus und die Sunder* (P. Lang, Frankfurt / M., 1976).

Forestall, C.S.B., J. T. *Targumic Traditions and the New Testament* (SBL Aramaic Studies 4, Chico: Scholars, 1979).

Freyne, S. *The World of the New Testament* (Michael Glazier, Inc., 1980).

Harrington, S. J., D. *God's People in Christ* (Fortress, 1980).

Juel, D. *Messiah and Temple: The Trial of Jesus in the Gospel of Mark* (SBL Dissertation Series, Scholars Press, 1979).

Klein, C. *Anti-Judaism in Christian Theology* (Fortress, 1978).

Koenig, J. *Jews and Christians in Dialogue: New Testament Foundations* (Westminster, 1979).

LeDeaut, R. *The Message of the New Testament and the Aramaic Bible* (Rome: Biblical Institute Press, 1982).

McNamara, M., *Targum and Testament* (Eerdmans, 1972).

Mussner, F. *Traktat uber die Juden* (Munich: Kosel, 1979). English translation by L. Swidler (1983).

Nickels, P. *Targum and New Testament: A Bibliography with a New Testament Index* (Scripta Pontifici Instituti Biblici, 117; Rome: Pontifical Biblical Institute, 1967).

Rivkin, E. *A Hidden Revolution: The Pharisees' Search for the Kingdom Within* (Abingdon, 1978).

Sanders, E. P. *Paul and Palestinian Judaism* (Fortress, 1977).

_____ ed., *Jewish and Christian Self-Definition* (Fortress, Vols. 1, 2, 1981).

Sandmel, S. *Anti-Semitism in the New Testament?* (Fortress, 1978).

_____ *Judaism and Christian Beginnings* (Oxford, 1978).

Sloyan, G. *Is Christ the End of the Law?* (Westminster, 1978).

_____ *Jesus on Trial* (Fortress, 1973).

_____ "Recent Literature on the Trial Narratives," T. J. Ryan, ed., *Critical History and Biblical Faith* (CTS, 1979, 136-176).

Stendahl, K. *Paul Among the Jews and Gentiles* (Fortress, 1976).

Thoma, C. *Christian Theology of Judaism* (Paulist, 1980).

Westermann, C. *Essays on Old Testament Hermeneutics* (1963).

Vermes, G. *Jesus the Jew* (Fontana/Collins, 1977).

In addition to these recent works, the classic texts of George Foot Moore, James Parkes, and W. D. Davies on rabbinic literature remain fundamental to the field.

C. LITURGY AND HOMILETICS

Bouyer, L., Jewish and Christian Liturgies" in L. Sheppard, ed., *True Worship* (Halcion Press, 1963).

Brickner, B. *An Interreligious Guide to Passover and Easter* (UAHC, 830 Fifth Avenue, New York, NY 10021), $1.00.

Cavalleti, S., "Christian Liturgy: Its Roots in Judaism," *SIDIC* (1973) 10-28.

Finkel, A., "The Passover Story and the Last Supper," in M. Zeik and M. Siegel, eds., *Root and Branch* (Roth, 1973) 19-46.

Finkel, A. and Frizzell, L. *Standing Before God: Studies in Prayer in Scriptures and Tradition* (KTAV, 1981).

Fisher, E. "The Liturgy of Lent and Christian-Jewish Relations," *Ecumenical Trends* (March 1981, 36-40).

_____ and Polish, D., eds. *Liturgical Foundations of Social Policy in the Catholic and Jewish Traditions* (University of Notre Dame Press, 1982).

Flusser, D., "Easter and the Passover Haggadah," *Immanuel* (1977) 52-61.

Idelsohn, A. *Jewish Liturgy an Its Development* (Schocken, 1967).

Klenicki, L., ed. *The Passover Celebration: A Haggadah for the Seder* (Anti-Defamation League / Archdiocese of Chicago, 1980).

LeDeaut, R., et al., *The Spirituality of Judaism* (Abbey Press, 1977).

McEvoy, D. *A Christian Service of Holocaust Remembrance* (National Conference of Christians and Jews, 1979).

_____ *Christians Confront the Holocaust: A Collection of Sermons* (National Conference of Christians and Jews, 1980).

Oesterley, W. O., *The Jewish Background of the Christian Liturgy* (Clarendon, Oxford, 1925).

Petuchowski, J. and Brocke, M., eds. *The Lord's Prayer and Jewish Liturgy* (Seabury, 1978).

Rijk, C. A. *Jewish and Christian Liturgy* (Special Editions, *SIDIC* Journal, Rome, Vols. VI, VIII, no. 1).

Simpson, W. *Light and Rejoicing: A Christian's Understanding of Jewish Worship* (Belfast, 1976).

Sloyan, G. *A Commentary on the New Lectionary* (Paulist, 1975).

Stendahl, K. "Holy Week" (in the series *Proclamation: Aids for Interpreting the Lessons of the Church Year*, Fortress, 1974).

Talley, T., "From Berekah to Eucharistia," *Worship* (Vol. 50:2, 1976) 115-137.

Werner, E. *The Sacred Bridge: Liturgical Parallels in the Synagogue and the Early Church* (Schocken, 1970).

D. HISTORY: CHURCH AND SYNAGOGUE

American Jewish Committee. *The Many Faces of Anti-Semitism* (1978).

_____ *About the Holocaust* (1980).

Bea, A. *The Church and the Jewish People* (Harper and Row, 1966).

Berger, D. *The Jewish-Christian Debate in the High Middle Ages* (Jewish Publication Society, 1979).

Broybrook, M. *Inter-Faith Organizations, 1893-1979: An Historical Survey* (Edwin Mellin Press, 1980).

Cargas, H. J. *A Christian Response to the Holocaust* (Stonehenge, 1982).

Chazan, R. *Church, State and Jew in the Middle Ages* (documents and commentary, Bohrman House, 1980).

Dawidowicz, L. *The War Against the Jews* (Holt, Reinhart and Winston, 1975).

Eckardt, A. "The Holocaust: Christian and Jewish Responses," *Journal of the American Academy of Religion*, September, 1974.

Feldblum, E. *The American Catholic Press and the Jewish State, 1917-1959* (KTAV, 1977).

Fisher, E. "Ani Ma'amin: Directions in Holocaust Theology," *Interface* (BCEIA, Winter 1980).

_____ "The Holocaust and Christian Responsibility," *America* (February, 14, 1981).

Flannery, E. *The Anguish of the Jews* (Macmillan, 1965).

Graham, R., *Pius XII's Defense of Jews: 1944-45* (Catholic League for Religious and Civil Rights, 1982).

Mendes-Flohr, P. and Reinharz, J. *The Jew in the Modern World: A Documentary History* (Oxford University, 1980).

Friedlander, H. and Milton, S. *The Holocaust: Ideology, Bureaucracy, Genocide* (Kraus International Publications, 1980).

Friedman, P. *Their Brothers' Keepers* (New York: Holocaust Library, 1978).

Hay, M. *The Roots of Christian Anti-Semitism* (Freedom Library Press, 1981).

Helmreich, E. C. *The German Churches Under Hitler* (Wayne State University, 1979).

Hertzberg, A. *The Zionist Idea* (Atheneum, 1973).

Jacob, W. *Christianity Through Jewish Eyes* (Hebrew Union College, 1974).

Jocz, J. *The Jewish People and Jesus Christ* (London: SPCK, 1954).

Kadushin, M. *The Rabbinic Mind* (Blaisdell, 1965).

de Lange, N. *Origen and the Jews* (University of Cambridge, 1976).

Lichten, J. *Pius XII and the Jews* (NCWC, 1963).

Littell, F. and Locke, H. *The German Church Struggle and the Holocaust* (Wayne State University, 1974).

Lewy, G. *The Catholic Church and Nazi Germany* (Wayne State University, 1974).

Montefiore, C. G. and Loewe, H. *A Rabbinic Anthology* (Schocken, 1974).

Morley, F. *Vatican Diplomacy and the Jews During the Holocaust 1939-43* (KTAV, 1980).

Neusner, J. *Understanding Jewish Theology* (KTAV / ADL, 1973).

_____ *Between Time and Eternity: The Essentials of Judaism* (Dickenson, 1975).

_____ *Understanding Rabbinic Judaism* (KTAV / ADL, 1974).

Newman, L. I. *Jewish Influence on Christian Reform Movements* (Columbia University, 1925).

Peck, J., ed., *Jews and Christians After the Holocaust* (Fortress, 1982).

Pelikan, J. *The Christian Tradition, Vol. 1: The Emergence of the Catholic Tradition* (110-600). The first two chapters are an excellent discussion of the split between Judaism and Christianity (University of Chicago Press, 1971).

Poliakov, L. *The History of Anti-Semitism* (Schocken, Volumes I, II, III, IV, 1965).

Rhodes, A. *The Vatican in the Age of the Dictators, 1922-1945* (Holt, Reinhart and Winston, 1973).

Roth, L. *Judaism: A Portrait* (Schocken, 1972).

Rudavsky, D. *Emancipation and Adjustment* (Diplomatic, 1967).

Ryan, M. D., ed. *Human Responses to the Holocaust* (Edwin Mellen Press, 1981).

Sachor, H. *The Course of Modern Jewish History* (Delta, 1958).

Schechter, S. *The Aspects of Rabbinic Theology* (Schocken, 1961).

Scholem, G. *The Messianic Idea in Judaism* (Schocken, 1971).

Schussler Fiorenza, E. *Aspects of Religious Propaganda in Judaism and Early Christianity* (University of Notre Dame, 1976).

Schweitzer, F. *A History of the Jews* (Macmillan, 1971). (See "Biographical Note," 306-312).

Shur, I. and Littell, F., eds. *Reflections on the Holocaust* (Annals of the American Academy of Political and Social Science, July 1980).

Stylianopoulos, T. *Justin Martyr and the Mosaic Law* (SBC Dissertation Series 20; Scholars, 1975).

Synan, E. *The Popes and the Jews in the Middle Ages* (Macmillan, 1965).

Talmage, F. E. *Disputation and the Dialogue* (ADL/KTAV, 1975).

Townsend, J. T., et al. *The Study of Judaism: Bibliographical Essays* (Volumes I, II; ADL, 1972, 1976).

Wiesel, E. *Night* (Avon, 1969).

Wilken, R. L. *Judaism and the Early Christian Mind* (Yale University, 1971).

_____, ed. *Aspects of Wisdom in Judaism and Early Christianity* (University of Notre Dame Press, 1975).

Wytwycky, B. *The Other Holocaust* (Wash., D.C.: Novack Report, 1980).

Yerushalmi, Y., *et al. Bibliographical Essays in Medieval Jewish Studies* (ADL/KTAV, 1976).

Zahn, G. *German Catholics and Hitler's Wars* (Sheed and Ward, 1962).

E. CATECHETICS

Biemer, G. *Frieburger Leitlinien zum Lernprozeses Christen-Juden* (Patmost, 1981).

Bishop, C. H. *How Catholics Look at Jews* (Paulist, 1974).

Fiedler, P. *Das Judentum in Katholischen Religions-unterricht* (Patmos Verlag, Dusseldorf, 1980).

Fisher, E., *Faith Without Prejudice* (Paulist, 1977).

Fisher, E. *Homework for Christians Preparing for Christian-Jewish Dialogue* (NCCJ, revised, 1982).

_____ "Dialogue: From Theology to the Classroom," *Origins* (Vol. II:11; Aug. 27, 1982) 167-176.

Isaac, J. *The Teaching of Contempt* (Holt, Reinhart and Winston, 1964).

_____ *Jesus and Israel* (Holt, Reinhart and Winston, 1971).

Lapide, P. *Israelis, Jews and Jesus* (Doubleday, 1979). Reports on the treatment of Christianity in Jewish textbooks and thought.

Olson, B. *Faith and Prejudice* (Yale University, 1963).

Long, J. G. *Judaism and the Christian Seminary Curriculum* (Loyola University Press, 1966).

Pawlikowski, J. *Catechetics and Prejudice* (Paulist, 1973).

Strober, G. *Portrait of the Elder Brother* (AJC, 1972).

Zerin, E. *What Catholics and Other Christians Should Know About Jews* (Wm. C. Brown, 1980).

The Secretariat for Catholic-Jewish Relations and Anti-Defamation League of the B'nai B'rith have jointly published two works for Catholic educators. *Abraham, Our Father in Faith* (1980) is a curriculum guide for integrating Christian-Jewish concerns into existing courses K to 12. *Understanding the Jewish Experience* provides sample models for in-service training programs for Catholic teachers. Together with Rabbi Leon Klenicki, E. Fisher has published a series of high school curriculum articles in *PACE (Professional Approaches for Christian Educators)* 1977-1983. See also the special edition of *SIDIC*, "Images of the Other: Presenting Judaism in Christian Education, Christianity in Jewish Education," Vol. 15:2, 1982.

F. JEWISH-CHRISTIAN RELATIONS (GENERAL AND THEOLOGICAL)

Banki, J., "The Church and the Jews: The Struggle at Vatican Council II," in *The American Jewish Yearbook* (American Jewish Committee: 1965 and 1966). The *Yearbook* is a basic resource document for information about the Jewish community.

Borowitz, E. *Contemporary Christologies: A Jewish Response (Paulist, 1980).*

Bokser, Z. *Judaism and the Christian Predicament* (Knopf, 1967).

van Buren, P. *Discerning the Way: A Theology of the Jewish-Christian Reality* (Seabury Crossroad, 1980).

Cohen, A. *The Myth of the Judeo-Christian Tradition* (Harper and Row, 1970).

Croner, H. and Klenicki, L. *Issues in the Jewish-Christian Dialogue: Jewish Perspectives on Covenant, Mission and Witness* (Paulist Stimulus, 1979).

Davies, A. T., ed. *Antisemitism and the Foundations of Christianity* (Paulist, 1979).

Drinan, R. F. *Honor the Promise* (Doubleday, 1977).

Eckardt, A. Roy. *Elder and Younger Brothers* (Schocken, 1973).

_____ *Your People, My People* (New York Times Book, 1974).

_____ and Eckardt, A. *A Long Night's Journey into Day: Life and Faith After the Holocaust* (Wayne State University, 1982).

Finkel, A. and Frizzell, L., eds., *Standing Before God: Studies in Prayer in Scriptures and Tradition with Essays in Honor of John M. Oesterreicher* (KTAV, 1981).

Fisher, E. *Faith Without Prejudice* (Paulist, 1977).

_____ *Homework for Christians Preparing for Jewish-Christian Dialogue* (National Conference of Christians and Jews, 1982).

_____ and Polish, D., eds., *Formation of Social Policy in the Catholic-Jewish Traditions* (University of Notre Dame Press, 1980).

Fleischner, E., ed. *Auschwitz, Beginning of a New Era?* (ADL/KTAV, 1977).

Hargrove, R.S.C.J., K. *The Star and the Cross: Essays on Jewish-Catholic Relations* (Milwaukee: Bruce, 1966).

Isaac, J. *Jesus and Israel* (Holdt, Rinehart and Winston, 1971).

Lacocque, A. *The Question of Election in the Life of God's People Today* (Knox, 1979).

Littell, F. *The Crucifixion of the Jews* (Harper and Row, 1975).

Oesterreicher, J. M., ed. *The Bridge* (Volumes I-V, Herder, 1955-1970).

Opsahl, D. and Tanenbaum, M., eds. *Speaking of God Today: Jews and Lutherans in Conversation* (Fortress, 1974).

Pawlikowski, J. *The Challenge of the Holocaust for Christian Theology* (ADL, 1978).

_____ *Sinai and Calvary* (Benzinger, 1976).

_____ *What Are They Saying About Christian-Jewish Relations?* (Paulist, 1980).

_____ *Christ in the Light of the Christian-Jewish Dialogue* (Paulist, 1982).

Rudin, A. J. *Israel for Christians* (Fortress, 1982).

Swidler, L., ed. *Jews and Christians in Dialogue* (Special Issue, *Journal of Ecumenical Studies*, Vol. 12:4, Fall 1975).

Tanenbaum, M. *et al. Evangelicals and Jews in Conversation* (Baker, 1978).

Thompson, N. and Cole, B., eds., *The Future of Jewish-Christian Relations* (Schenectady, N.Y.: Character Research Press, 1982).

Vaporis, N. and Tanenbaum, M., eds. "Greek Orthodox-Jewish Consultation," (Special Issue, *The Greek Orthodox Theological Review*, Vol. 22:1, Spring 1977).

Zeik, M. and Siegel, M., eds. *Root and Branch* (Roth, 1973).

Appendices

APPENDIX A

Second Vatican Council

THE DECLARATION ON THE RELATION OF
THE CHURCH TO NON-CHRISTIAN RELIGIONS (NOSTRA AETATE):
AAS 58 (1966), PP. 740-744. HERE, NOS. 4-5.
ENGLISH: SPCU TRANSLATION.*

*With permission from *Doing the Truth in Charity*, ed. by T. F. Stransky, CSP, and J. B. Sheerin, CSP (Paulist, 1982), which contains the basic official documentation from 1964-1980 (pp. 339-358).

As the Council searches into the mystery of the Church, it remembers the spiritual bonds which ties the people of the New Covenant to the offspring of Abraham.

Thus the Church of Christ acknowledges that, according to God's saving design, the beginnings of her faith and her election are found already in the patriarchs, Moses and the prophets. She professes that all who believe in Christ—Abraham's sons according to the faith (cf. Gal. 3, 7)—are included in this patriarch's call, and likewise that the salvation of the Church is symbolically prefigured in the exodus of the chosen people from the land of bondage. The Church, therefore, cannot forget that she received the revelation of the Old Testament through the people with whom God in his inexpressible mercy made the ancient covenant. Nor can she forget that she draws sustenance from the root of that well-cultivated olive tree onto which have been grafted the wild shoots, the Gentiles (cf. Rom. 11, 17-24). Indeed, the Church believes that by his cross Christ, who is our Peace, reconciled Jews and Gentiles, making the two one in himself (cf. Eph. 2, 14-16).

The Church keeps ever in mind the words of the Apostle about his kinsmen: "Theirs is the sonship and the glory and the covenant and the law and the worship and the promises; theirs are the fathers and from them is the Christ according to the flesh" (Rom. 9, 4-5), the Son of the Virgin Mary. She also recalls that the apostles, the Church's foundation-stones and pillars, as well as most of the early disciples who proclaimed the Gospel of Christ to the world, sprang from the Jewish people.

As Holy Scripture testifies, Jerusalem did not recognize the time of her visitation (cf. Luke 19, 44), nor did the Jews, in large number, accept the Gospel; indeed, not a few of them opposed its dissemination (cf. Rom. 11, 28). Nevertheless, now as before, God holds the Jews most dear for the sake of their fathers; he does not repent of the gifts he makes or of the calls he issues—such is the witness of the Apostle (cf. Rom. 11, 28-29; also cf. *Dogmatic Constitution on the Church: AAS* 57 [1965], p. 20). In company with the prophets and the same Apostle, the Church awaits that day, known to God alone, on which all peoples will address the Lord with a single voice and "serve him with one accord" (Soph. 3, 9; cf. Is. 66, 23; Ps. 65, 4; Rom. 11, 11-32).

Since the spiritual patrimony common to Christians and Jews is then so rich, the Council wishes to foster and commend mutual understanding and esteem. This will be the fruit, above all, of biblical and theological studies and of brotherly dialogues.

True, the Jewish authorities and those who followed their lead pressed for the death of Christ (cf. John 19, 6); still, what happened in his passion cannot be charged against all the Jews, without distinction, then alive, nor against the Jews of today. Although the Church is the new People of God, the Jews should not be represented as rejected by God or accursed, as if this followed from Holy Scripture. All should see to it, then, that in catechetical work and in the preaching of the Word of God they teach nothing save what conforms to the truth of the Gospel and the spirit of Christ.

The Church, moreover, rejects every persecution against any person. For this reason and for the sake of the patrimony she shares with the Jews, the Church decries hatreds, persecutions and manifestations of anti-Semitism directed against Jews at any time and by anyone. She does so, not impelled by political reasons, but moved by the spiritual love of the Gospel.

Besides, Christ underwent his passion and death freely and out of infinite love because of the sins of men in order that all might reach salvation. This the Church has always taught and teaches still; it is therefore the duty of the Church to proclaim the cross of Christ as the sign of God's all-embracing love and as the fountain from which every grace flows.

We cannot truly call upon God, the Father of all, if we refuse to treat in a brotherly way any class of people, created as all are in the image of God. Man's relation to God, the Father, and his relation to men, his brothers, are so linked together that Scripture says: 'He who does not love does not know God" (1 John 4, 8).

No foundation therefore remains for any theory or practice that leads to discrimination between man and man or people and people insofar as their human dignity and the rights flowing from it are concerned.

The Church reproves, as foreign to the mind of Christ, any discrimination against persons or harrassment of them because of their race, color, condition in life or religion. On the contrary, following the footsteps of the holy apostles Peter and Paul, the Council ardently implores the Christian faithful to "maintain good fellowship among the nations" (1 Pet. 2, 12) and, if possible, to live for their part in peace with all men (cf. Rom. 12, 18), so that they may truly be sons of the Father who is in heaven (cf. Matt. 5, 45).

APPENDIX B

Commission for Religious Relations with the Jews

GUIDELINES AND SUGGESTIONS
FOR IMPLEMENTING THE CONCILIAR
DECLARATION "NOSTRA AETATE" (n. 4)

INTRODUCTORY NOTE

The document is published over the signature of Cardinal Willebrands, in his capacity as President of the Commission for the Catholic Church's religious relations with the Jews, instituted by Paul VI on 22 October 1974. It comes out a short time after the ninth anniversary of the promulgation of Nostra Aetate, the Second Vatican Council's Declaration on the Church's relations with non-Christian religions.

The "Guidelines and Suggestions", which refer to n. 4 of the Declaration, are notable for their almost exclusively practical nature and for their sobriety.

This deliberately practical nature of the text is justified by the fact that it concerns a pragmatic document.

It does not propose a Christian theology of Judaism. Such a theology certainly has an interest for specialist research and reflection, but it still needs considerable study. The new Commission for Religious Relations with the Jews should be able to play a part in the gradual fruition of this endeavour.

The first part of the Document recalls the principal teachings of the Council on the condemnation of antisemitism and of all discrimination, and the obligation of reciprocal understanding and of renewed mutual esteem. It also hopes for a better knowledge on the part of Christians of the essence of the religious tradition of Judaism and of the manner in which Jews identify themselves.

The text then proposes a series of concrete suggestions.

The section dedicated to dialogue *calls for fraternal dialogue and the establishment of deep doctrinal research. Prayer in common is also proposed as a means of encounter.*

With regard to the liturgy, *mention is made of the links between the Christian liturgy and the Jewish liturgy and of the caution which is needed in dealing with commentaries on biblical texts, and with liturgical explanations and translations.*

The part concerning teaching and education *allows the relations between the two Testaments to be made clear. The question of the trial and death of Jesus is also touched upon and stress is laid on the note of expectation which characterizes both the Jewish and the Christian religion. Specialists are invited to conduct serious research and the establishment of chairs of Hebrew studies is encouraged where it is possible, as well as collaboration with Jewish scholars.*

The final section deals with the possibilities of common social action *in the context of a search for social justice and for peace.*

The conclusion *touches on, among other things, the ecumenical aspect of the problem of relations with Judaism, the initiatives of local churches in this area, and the essential lines of the mission of the new Commission instituted by the Holy See.*

The great sobriety of the text is noted also in the concrete suggestions which it puts forward. But it would certainly be wrong to interpret such sobriety as being indicative of a limiting programme of activities. The document does propose limited suggestions for some key sectors, but it is a document meant for the universal Church, and as such it cannot take account of all the individual situations. The suggestions put forward are intended to give ideas to those who were asking themselves how to start on a local level that dialogue which the text invites them to begin and to develop. These suggestions are mentioned because of their value as examples. They are made because it seems that they could find ample application and that their proposal at the same time constitutes an apt program for aiding local churches to organize their own activities, in order to harmonize with the general movement of the universal Church in dialogue with Judaism.

The Document can be considered from a certain point of view as the Commission's first step for the realization of religious relations with Judaism. It will devolve on the new Commission to prepare and put forward, when necessary, the further developments which may seem necessary in order that the initiative of the Second Vatican Council in this important area may continue to bear fruit on a local level and on a worldwide level, for the benefit of peace of heart and harmony of spirit of all who work under the protection of the one Almighty God.

The Document can be considered from a certain point of view as the Commission's first step for the realization of religious relations with Judaism. It will devolve on the Commission to prepare and put forward, when necessary, the further developments which may seem necessary in order that the initiative of the Second Vatican Council in this important area may continue to bear fruit on a local level and on a worldwide level, for the benefit of peace of heart and harmony of spirit of all who work under the protection of the one Almighty God.

Preamble

The Declaration *Nostra Aetate*, issued by the Second Vatican Council on 28 October 1965, "on the relationship of the Church to non-Christian religions" (n. 4), marks an important milestone in the history of Jewish-Christian relations.

Moreover, the step taken by the Council finds its historical setting in circumstances deeply affected by the memory of the persecution and massacre of Jews which took place in Europe just before and during the Second World War.

Although Christianity sprang from Judaism, taking from it certain essential elements of its faith and divine cult, the gap dividing them was deepened more and more, to such an extent that Christian and Jew hardly knew each other.

After two thousand years, too often marked by mutual ignorance and frequent confrontation, the Declaration *Nostra Aetate* provides an opportunity to open or to continue a dialogue with a view to better mutual understanding. Over the past nine years, many steps in this direction have been taken in various countries. As a result, it is easier to distinguish conditions under which a new relationship between Jews and Christians may be worked out and developed. This seems the right moment to propose, following the guidelines of the Council, some concrete suggestions born of experience, hoping that they will help to bring into actual existence in the life of the Church the intentions expressed in the conciliar document.

While referring the reader back to this document, we may simply restate here that the spiritual bonds and historical links binding the Church to Judaism condemn (as opposed to the very spirit of Christianity) all forms of anti-semitism and discrimination, which in any case the dignity of the human person alone would suffice to condemn. Further still, these links and relationships render obligatory a better mutual understanding and renewed mutual esteem. On the practical level in particular, Christians must therefore strive to acquire a better knowledge of the basic components of the religious tradition of Judaism; they must strive to learn by what essential traits the Jews define themselves in the light of their own religious experience.

With due respect for such matters of principle, we simply propose some first practical applications in different essential areas of the Church's life, with a view to launching or developing sound relations between Catholics and their Jewish brothers.

I. Dialogue

To tell the truth, such relations as there have been between Jew and Christian have scarcely ever risen above the level of monologue. From now on, real dialogue must be established.

Dialogue presupposes that each side wishes to know the other, and wishes to increase and deepen its knowledge of the other. It constitutes a particularly suitable means of favouring a better mutual knowledge and, especially in the case of dialogue between Jews and Christians, of probing the riches of one's own tradition. Dialogue demands respect for the other as he is; above all, respect for his faith and his religious convictions.

In virtue of her divine mission, and her very nature, the Church must preach Jesus Christ to the world *(Ad Gentes, 2)*. Lest the witness of Catholics to Jesus Christ should give offence to Jews, they must take care to live and spread their Christian faith while maintaining the strictest respect for religious liberty in line with the teachings of the Second Vatican Council (Declaration *Dignitatis Humanae)*. They will likewise strive to understand the difficulties which arise for the Jewish soul—rightly imbued with an extremely high, pure notion of the divine transcendence—when faced with the mystery of the incarnate Word.

While it is true that a widespread air of suspicion, inspired by and unfortunate past, is still dominant in this particular area, Christians, for their part, will be able to see to what extent the responsibility is theirs and deduce practical conclusions for the future.

In addition to friendly talks, competent people will be encouraged to meet and to study together the many problems deriving from the fundamental convictions of Judaism and of Christianity. In order not to hurt (even involuntarily) those taking part, it will be vital to guarantee, not only tact, but a great openness of spirit and diffidence with respect to one's own prejudices.

In whatever circumstances as shall prove possible and mutually acceptable, one might encourage a common meeting in the presence of God, in prayer and silent meditation, a highly efficacious way of finding that humility, that openness of heart and mind, necessary prerequisites for a deep knowledge of oneself and of others. In particular, that will be done in connection with great causes such as the struggle for peace and justice.

II. Liturgy

The existing links between the Christian liturgy and the Jewish liturgy will be borne in mind. The idea of a living community in the service of God, and in the service of men for the love of God, such as this service is realized in the liturgy, is just as characteristic of the Jewish liturgy as it is of the Christian one. To improve Jewish-Christian relations, it is important to take cognizance of those common elements of the liturgical life (formulas, feasts, rites, etc.) in which the Bible holds as essential place.

An effort will be made to acquire a better understanding of whatever in the Old Testament retains its own perpetual value (cf. *Dei Verbum*, 14-15), since that has not been cancelled by the later interpretation of the New Testament. Rather, the New Testament brings out the full meaning of the Old, while both Old and New illumine and explain each other (cf. *ibid.*, 16). This is all the more important since liturgical reform is now bringing the text of the Old Testament ever more frequently to the attention of Christians.

When commenting on biblical texts, emphasis will be laid on the continuity of our faith with that of the earlier Covenant, in the perspective of the promises, without minimizing those elements of Christianity which are original. We believe that those promises were fulfilled with the first coming of Christ. But it is none the less true that we still await their perfect fulfillment in his glorious return at the end of time.

With respect to liturgical readings, care will be taken to see that homilies based on them will not distort their meaning, especially when it is a question of passages which seem to show the Jewish people as such in an unfavorable light. Efforts will be made so to instruct the Christian people that they will understand the true interpretation of all the texts and their meaning for the contemporary believer.

Commissions entrusted with the task of liturgical translation will pay particular attention to the way in which they express those phrases and passages which Christians, if not well informed, might misunderstand because of prejudice. Obviously, one cannot alter the text of the Bible. The point is that, with a version destined for liturgical use, there should be an overriding preoccupation to bring out explicitly the meaning of a text[1] while taking scriptural studies into account.

The preceding remarks also apply to introductions to biblical readings, to the Prayer of the Faithful, and to commentaries printed in missals used by the laity.

III. Teaching and Education

Although there is still a great deal of work to be done, a better understanding of Judaism itself and its relationship to Christianity has been achieved in recent years thanks to the teaching of the Church, the study and research of scholars, and also to the beginning of dialogue.

In this respect, the following facts deserve to be recalled.

—It is the same God, "inspirer and author of the books of both Testaments," *(Dei Verbum*, 16), who speaks both in the old and new Covenants.

—Judaism in the time of Christ and the Apostles was a complex reality, embracing many different trends, many spiritual, religious, social and cultural values.

—The Old Testament and the Jewish tradition founded upon it must not be set against the New Testament in such as way that the former seems to constitute a religion of only justice, fear and legalism, with no appeal to the love of God and neighbour (cf. *Deut.* 6:5, *Lev.* 19:18, *Matt.* 22:34-40).

—Jesus was born of the Jewish people, as were his Apostles and a large number of his first disciples. When he revealed himself as the Messiah and Son of God (cf. *Matt.* 16:16), the bearer of the new Gospel message, he did so as the fulfillment and perfection of the earlier Revelation. And, although his teaching had profoundly new character, Christ, nevertheless, in many instances, took his stand on the teaching of the Old Testament. The New Testament is profoundly marked by its relation to the Old. As the Second Vatican Council declared: "God, the inspirer and author of the books of both Testaments, wisely arranged that the New Testament be hidden in the Old and the Old be made manifest in the New" *(Dei Verbum,* 16). Jesus also used teaching methods similar to those employed by the rabbis of his time.

Thus the formula "the Jews", in St. John, sometimes according to the context means "the leaders of the Jews", or "the adversaries of Jesus", terms which express better the thought of the evangelist and avoid appearing to arraign the Jewish people as such. Another example is the use of the words "pharisee" and "pharisaism" which have taken on a largely pejorative meaning.

—With regard to the trial and death of Jesus, the Council recalled that "what happened in his passion cannot be blamed upon all the Jews then living, without distinction, nor upon the Jews of today" *(Nostra Aetate,* 4).

—The history of Judaism did not end with the destruction of Jerusalem, but rather went on to develop a religious tradition. And, although we believe that the importance and meaning of that tradition were deeply affected by the coming of Christ, it is still nonetheless rich in religious values.

—With the prophets and the apostle Paul, "the Church awaits the day, known to God alone, onwhich all peoples will address the Lord in a single voice and 'serve him with one accord' *(Soph.* 3:9)" *(Nostra Aetate,* 4).

Information concerning these questions is important at all levels of Christian instruction and education. Among sources of information special attention should be paid to the following:
—catechisms and religious textbooks;
—history books;
—the mass-media (press, radio, cinema, television).

The effective use of these means presupposes the thorough formation of instructors and educators in training schools, seminaries and universities.

Research into the problems bearing on Judaism and Jewish-Christian relations will be encouraged among specialists, particularly in the fields of exegesis, theology, history and sociology. Higher institutions of Catholic research, in association if possible with other similar Christian institutions and experts, are invited to contribute to the solution of such problems. Wherever possible, chairs of Jewish studies will be created and collaboration with Jewish scholars encouraged.

IV. Joint Social Action

Jewish and Christian tradition, founded on the Word of God, is aware of the value of the human person, the image of God. Love of the same God must show itself in effective action for the good of mankind. In the spirit of the prophets, Jews and Christians will work willingly together, seeking social justice and peace at every level—local, national and international.

At the same time, such collaboration can do much to foster mutual understanding and esteem.

Conclusion

The Second Vatican Council has pointed out the path to follow in promoting deep fellowship between Jews and Christians. But there is still a long road ahead.

The problem of Jewish-Christian relations concerns the Church as such, since it is when "pondering her own mystery" that she encounters the mystery of Israel. Therefore, even in areas where no Jewish communities exist, this remains an important problem. there is also an ecumenical aspect to the question: the very return of Christians to the source and origins of their faith, grafted on to the earlier Covenant, helps the search for unity in Christ, the cornerstone.

In this field, the bishops will know what best to do on the pastoral level, within the general disciplinary framework of the Church and in line with the common teaching of her magisterium. For example, they will create some suitable commissions or secretariats on a national or regional level, or appoint some competent person to promote the implementation of hte conciliar directives and the suggestions made above.

On 22 October 1974, the Holy Father instituted for the universal Church this Commission for Religious Relations with the Jews, joined to the Secretariat for Promoting Christian Unity. This special Commission, created to encourage and foster religious relations between Jews and Catholics—and to do so eventually in collaboration with other Christians—will be, within the limits of its competence, at the service of all interested organizations, providing information for them, and helping them to pursue their task in conformity with the instructions of the Holy See.

The Commission wishes to develop this collaboration in order to implement, correctly and effectively, the express intentions of the Council.

Given at Rome, 1 December 1974.

> Johannes Card. Willebrands
> *President of the Commission*

> Pierre-Marie de Contenson, O.P.
> *Secretary of the Commission*

APPENDIX C

John Paul II

Dialogue: The Road to Understanding

Jewish-Catholic dialogue "takes on a quite special value in the dark background of the persecution and attempted elimination of the Jewish people in this country," Pope John Paul II told representatives of the German Jewish community at a meeting Nov. 17, 1980 in Mainz. The innocent victims of the Holocaust, he said, are tragic demonstrations of where "discrimination and contempt for human dignity can lead." The Pope praised the efforts by German Jews and Catholics to build bridges between their traditions. "It is not only a question of correcting a false religious view of the Jewish people...but...a question of the dialogue between the two religions which—with Islam—can give to the world the belief in one ineffable God who speaks to us and which...wish to serve him." An NC News translation of his address follows.

Reprinted with permission from *Origins* (12/4/80).

I thank you for the friendly and sincere words of greeting. This meeting was my desire on the occasion of this apostolic visit and I thank you for responding to my wish. May God's blessing stand over us in this hour.

1. If Christians see each other as brothers and must treat each other accordingly, how much more should this be true when they stand before the Jewish people.

In the "Declaration on the Relations of the Church to Judaism" in April of this year, the bishops of the Federal Republic of Germany began: "Who meets Jesus Christ, meets Judaism." May I make these words my own.

The faith of the church in Jesus Christ, the son of David and son of Abraham (Mt. 1:1) contains in reality what the bishops in their declaration call the spiritual legacy of Israel for the church" (Section II), a living legacy that must be understood and treasured in its profundity and its richness.

2. The concrete brotherly relation between Jews and Catholics in Germany takes on a quite special value in the dark background of the persecution and attempted elimination of the Jewish people in this country.

The innocent victims in Germany and elsewhere, the detroyed or dispersed families, the irretrievably lost cultural values and art treasures are a tragic demonstration of where discrimination and contempt for human dignity can lead, especially when this is inspired by perverse theories of the alleged differences in the values of races or the division of mankind into "worthy" and "worthy of life," as opposed to "without value" and unworthy of life." Before God all men are equally worthy and important.

In this spirit, Christians during the persecution worked, often in danger, to prevent the suffering of their Jewish brothers or to moderate them. I extend to them, at this time, my recognition and thanks.

But there were also others who as Christians went to the end in the affirmation of their adherence to the Jewish people along the road of suffering with their brothers and sisters. Such was the great Edith Stein, in religion Theresa Benedicta of the Cross, whose memory is held justly in high honor.

I would also like to mention Franz Rosenzweig and Martin Buber, who through their creative familiarity with the Hebrew and with the German languages established a truly admirable bridge for a profound encounter between the two cultures.

You yourselves in your greetings mentioned that among the many efforts to create a new common life with Jewish fellow citizens, Catholics and the church have made decisive contributions. This recognition and the corresponding necessary cooperation on your part fills me with joy.

On my part, I must express my grateful admiration for your own related initiatives, including the recent creation of your institute of higher education in Heidelberg.

3. The depth and the richness of our common inheritance bring us together in a friendly dialogue and mutually trustful collaboration. I rejoice that this goes forward in this land conscientiously and with determination.

Many public and private initiatives in the pastoral, academic and social fields serve this end, for example, solemn occasions such as the recent *Katholikentag* in Berlin. An encouraging sign also was the meeting of the International Liason Committee of the Roman Catholic Church and Judaism in the past year in Regensburg.

In all this it is not only a question of correcting a false religious view of the Jewish people, which caused in part the misunderstandings and persecution in the course of history, but above all a question of the dialogue between the two religions which—with Islam—can give to the world the belief in one ineffable God who speaks to us and which, representing the entire world, wish to serve him.

"The first dimension of this dialogue, that is the meeting between the people of God of the old covenant never retracted by God" (Rom. 11:29), on the one hand, and the people of the new covenant, on the other, is at the same time a dialogue within our own church, so to speak, a dialogue between the first and the second part of its Bible.

On this the "Directory for the Execution of the Conciliar Decree *Nostra Aetate*" states: "An effort will be made to acquire a better understanding of whatever in the Old Testament retains its own perpetual values...since that has not been cancelled by the later interpretation of the New Testament. Rather, the New Testament brings out the full meaning of the Old, while both Old and New illumine and explain each other" (II).

A second dimension of our dialogue—the real, central consideration—is the encounter between today's Christian churches and today's people of the covenant concluded with Moses. The postconciliar directive mentioned tells us how important it is that Christians tend to understand better the fundamental components of the religious tradition of Judaism and that they learn what fundamental lines are essential for the lived religious reality of Jews, according to their own understanding of it (Introduction).

The road to this reciprocal learning process is dialogue. I thank you, respected brothers, that you too lead the dialogue with the "opening and largeness of the spirit," with that "rhythm" and that prudence which were recommended to us Catholics by the above mentioned directives.

One result of this dialogue, and a sign pointing to its fruitful continuance, is the declaration of the German bishops already cited, "On the Relations of the Church to Judaism," of this past April. It is my earnest wish that this declaration becomes the spiritual property of all the Catholics of Germany!

I would like also to mention briefly a third dimension of our dialogue. The German bishops devote the concluding chapter of their declaration to the tasks that we have in common. Jews and Christians are called, as sons of Abraham, to be a blessing for the world (Gn. 12:2). They engage themselves jointly to work for peace and justice among all men and people and in the fullness and profundity that God himself has disposed for us and with readiness for the sacrifices that this high goal may impose on us. "The more this holy duty inspires our encounter, so much the more will it become for us a blessing."

4. In the light of this promise and this Abraham-like call I look with you toward the destiny and the role of your people among the peoples. I gladly pray with you for the fullness of *shalom* for all your brethren of the same faith and the same people and also for the land to which all Jews look with special reverence.

Our century witnessed the first pilgrimage of a pope in the Holy Land. Here, in concluding, I can repeat the words of Paul VI at his entrance into Jerusalem: "By your wishes and your prayers, invoke with us upon this land, unique in the world, which God has visited, his graces of concord and of peace. Let us here, all together, implore the grace of true profound brotherhood between all men and among all peoples...'May those who love you prosper! May peace be within your walls, prosperity in your buildings; I will say, Peace be within you!...I will pray for your good' (Ps. 122, 6-9)."

May all the peoples in Jerusalem be blessed and reconciled in Abraham. He, the ineffable, of whom all his creation speaks. He who does not constrain mankind to the good but guides it nevertheless. He who announces our destiny and is silent. He who has chosen us for all to his people. He who guides us on his roads in his future.

May his name be praised. Amen.

APPENDIX D

John Paul II

The Importance of Jewish-Christian Relations

Pope John Paul II stressed the importance of achieving "authentic, fruitful and lasting relationships with the Jewish people" in an address to experts in Christian-Jewish relations March 6, 1982. The experts were in Rome for an exchange of information among representatives of Catholic bishops' conferences and non-Catholic Christian churches. The "misunderstandings, errors and even insults," which have marked Christian-Jewish relations in the past must now be overcome with "understanding, peace and mutual esteem," he said. Christians are on the right path "when they seek, with respect and perseverance, to gather with their Semitic brethren around the common heritage which is a treasure to us all," although these efforts, he warned, should not lead to a loss of Christian identity. Dialogue with Jews enriches the church's knowledge of its own roots, he continued. "Our common heritage is considerable. Help in better understanding certain aspects of the church's life can be gained by taking an inventory of that heritage, but also by taking account of the faith and religious life of the Jewish people as professed and lived now as well." Catholic teaching and catechesis, he concluded, must reach the point where Jews and Judaism are not only presented "in an honest and objective manner, but will also do so without any prejudice or offense to anyone." An NC News translation of his French-language address follows.

Reprinted with permission from *Origins* (3/25/82).

You have gathered here in Rome from different parts of the world to explore the important matter of relations between the Catholic Church and Judaism. The importance of this problem is also emphasized by the presence among you of representatives of the Orthodox Churches, the Anglican Communion, the Lutheran World Federation and the World Council of Churches. I am glad to be able to greet all these especially and to thank them for their collaboration.

I likewise express all my gratitude to you who are bishops, priests, religious, Christian laity. Like your commitments in pastoral activities or in the field of biblical and theological research, your presence here shows the degree to which relations between the Catholic Church and Judaism touch on various aspects of the church and her activities.

This is easily understood. The Second Vatican Council said in its declaration on the church's relations with non-Christian religions, *Nostra Aetate* (no. 4): As this sacred synod searches into the mystery of the church, it recalls the spiritual bond linking the people of the new covenant with Abraham's stock." I myself have had occasion to say more than once: Our two religious communities "are linked at the very level of their identities" (cf. Discourse of March 12, 1979, to representatives of Jewish organizations and communities.) Indeed, and I again quote the text of the declaration *Nostra Aetate* (no. 4):

"The church of Christ acknowledges that, according to the mystery of God's saving design, the beginnings of her faith and her election are already found among the patriarchs, Moses, and the prophets...The church therefore cannot forget that she received the revelation of the Old Testament through this people...She ever keeps in mind the words of the apostle Paul about his kinsmen, 'who have the adoption as sons, and the glory, and the covenant and the legislation and the worship and the promises; who have the fathers, and from whom is Christ according to the flesh' (Rom. 9:4-5), the son of the Virgin Mary.''

This is as much as to say that the links between the church and the Jewish people are grounded in the design of the God of the covenant, and that as such, they have necessarily left traces in certain aspects of the church's institutions, especially in the liturgy.

Certainly since a new bough appeared from the common root, 2,000 years ago, we know that relations between our two communities have been marked by resentments and a lack of understanding. If there have been misunderstandings, errors and even insults since the day of separation, it is now a question of overcoming them with understanding, peace and mutual esteem. The terrible persecution suffered by the Jews in various periods of history have finally opened many eyes and disturbed many hearts. Thus Christians are on the right path, that of justice and brotherhood, when they seek, with respect and perseverance, to gather with their Semitic brethren around the common heritage which is a treasure to us all.

Is there any need to point out, above all to those who remain skeptical or even hostile, that such rapprochement should not be confused with a certain religious relativism, still less with a loss of identity? For their part, Christians profess their faith without equivocation in the universal salvific character of the death and resurrection of Jesus of Nazareth.

Yes, clarity and awareness of our Christian identity are an essential basis for achieving authentic, fruitful and lasting relationships with the Jewish people. I am happy to know that in this regard you are making many efforts, by studying and praying together, to grasp better and to formulate more clearly the often difficult biblical and theological problems raised by the progress of the Judeo-Christian dialogue. May God grant that Christians and Jews may hold more in-depth exchanges based on their own identities, without ever allowing either one or the other side to be obscured, but always seeking truly for the will of the God who revealed himself.

Such relationships can and ought to help enrich the knowledge of our own roots and to shed more light on certain aspects of this identity which we have. Our common spiritual heritage is considerable. Help in better understanding certain aspects of the church's life can be gained by taking an inventory of that heritage, but also by taking into account the faith and religious life of the Jewish people as professed and lived now as well. This is the case with the liturgy. Its roots have still to be more deeply traced, and above all need to be better known and appreciated by the faithful. This is true at the level of our institutions, for they have been inspired ever since the beginning of the church by certain aspects of the synagogue's community organization. Finally, our common spiritual patrimony is above all important at the level of our faith in one sole and unique God, who is good and merciful, who loves men and makes himself loved by them (cf. Song. 11:24-26), who is master of history and of men's destinies, who is our Father, and who chose Israel, ''that good olive tree onto which have been grafted the wild olive branches of the gentiles'' *(Nostra Aetate*, 4; cf. also Rom. 11:17-24).

This is why you have been concerned during your session with Catholic teaching and catechesis in regard to the Jews and Judaism. You have been guided on this point, as on others, and have been encouraged by the ''Guidelines and Suggestions for Implementing the Council Declaration *Nostra Aetate* (no. 4)," published by the Commission for Religious Relations with the Jews (cf. Chapter III). It is necessary to get to the point where such teaching at the various levels of religious instruction and in catechesis with children and adolescents will not only present the Jews and Judaism in an honest and objective manner, but will also do so without any prejudice or offense to anyone and, even more, with a lively awareness of that heritage that we have broadly outlined.

Finally, it is on such a basis that close collaboration will be able to be established—it is already making itself very happily felt. Our common heritage impels us toward this, our common heritage of service to man and his immense spiritual and material needs. We shall be able to go by diverse—but in the end, convergent—paths with the help of the Lord, who has never ceased loving his people (cf. Rom. 11:1), to reach true brotherhood in reconciliation, respect, and full accomplishment of God's plan in history.

I am happy to encourage you, dear brothers and sisters in Christ, to continue on the path you have taken, giving proof of your discernment and confidence, as well as your very great fidelity to the magisterium. In this way you provide an authentic service to the church, flowing from her mysterious vocation, and contribute to the good of the church, the Jewish people and all of mankind.

APPENDIX E

Archbishop John R. Roach

A Renewed Vision of Catholic-Jewish Relations

"Today, through dialogue, Christians are coming to realize that many of our previous assumptions about the nature of Judaism were, to put it kindly, wrong," Archbishop John Roach of St. Paul-Minneapolis told the executive committee of the Synagogue Council of America March 12, 1981. Roach, president of the National Conference of Catholic Bishops, said that until recently Christians tended to view "the spiritual legacy of Israel for the church" as a past reality abrogated by the coming of Christ and superseded by the Christian dispensation. "That such a view impoverishes Christianity as well as doing injustice to the integrity of Judaism is now increasingly recognized in our community," he said. Roach also analyzed the pope's address last fall to the German Jewish community. The text of his address follows.

Reprinted with permission from *Origins* (5/7/81).

Catholic-Jewish relations have progressed remarkably in the few years that have elapsed since the Second Vatican Council in its declaration, *Nostra Aetate*, called the church to a renewed vision of its ancient relationship with the Jewish people.

From the point of view of the church, this renewal in dialogue is much more than simply an exercise in good neighborliness. It is, as Pope John Paul II stated in his first meeting with representatives of the world Jewish community two years ago this month, a "solemn mandate," which reaches the essence of the Christian community's own self-understanding. "Thus," the pope declared, "it (is) understood that our two religious communities are connected and closely related at the very level of their respective religious identities" (NC News, March 15, 1979).

It must be admitted, in deep sorrow, that what the council called "the spiritual bond" linking our two peoples tended to slip from our awareness for long periods in centuries past. Often it was honored more in the breach than in the proper spirit of love. Yet since we believe the link to be divinely forged, out of the very election of our two peoples to serves God's will, the Christian must proclaim that it is a link which can never be wholly broken.

Today, through dialogue, Christians are coming to realize that many of our previous assumptions about the nature of Judaism were, to put it kindly, wrong. Thus we tended to cast what *Nostra Aetate* called, "the spiritual legacy of Israel for the church" almost exclusively in negative terms, deeming that legacy a past reality abrogated by the coming of Christ and superseded by the Christian dispensation. That such a view impoverishes Christianity as well as doing injustice to the integrity of Judaism is now increasingly recognized in our community (cf. "Statement on Catholic-Jewish Relations," National Conference of Catholic Bishops, Nov. 20, 1975). Indeed, the pope, in his most recent statement to the Jewish community on the occasion of his visit to Germany last fall, specifically interpreted *Nostra Aetate* as calling for an appreciation of Judaism as "a *living* legacy that must be understood by Christians "in its profundity and richness" (NC News, Nov. 20, 1980; italics added).

This statement of the pope in Germany, I believe, deserves closer attention than it has received to date. For in it the pope both consolidates insights gained from the dialogue and projects in a few short paragraphs his own vision of its structure and future possibilities.

The pope discerns three essential and interrelated dimensions in the dialogue. I would like to recall these with some particular references to the situation in our own country.

1. The first dimension flows from the past, from our common origins and the roots of Christianity in Judaism. From this perspective, the pope sees today's dialogue as "the meeting between the people of God of the old covenant never retracted by God (Rom. 11:29) on the one hand, and the people of the new covenant on the other." The phrase "never retracted by God" needs to be underscored. it at once rebuts all old claims of Christian triumphalism (the so-called "teaching of contempt") and opens up the way for an entirely new relationship between two living traditions on the basis of mutual respect for each other's essential religious claims.

Obviously this formulation does not answer all our questions about each other or, frankly, about ourselves. In this context the pope notes that the dialogue with Jews is "at the same time a dialogue within our own church, a dialogue between the first and second parts of its Bible." He cautions Catholics to hold fast to biblical values which "have not been obliterated by later interpretations of the New Testament (cf. "Guidelines and Suggestions for Implementing the Conciliar Decree, *Nostra Aetate*," Rome, Dec. 1, 1974)."

It is good to be able to note here the many dialogues taking place in this country on the academic levels which seek to plumb the mysteries of the unique covenant relationship between our two peoples. One such is the joint "Historical Reflection on the Notion of Covenant" which took place in Los Angeles in March of 1979. Others can be seen in the many dialogues sponsored on the national level by our own secretariat for Catholic-Jewish relations with a variety of Jewish and Protestant agencies.

2. The second dimension of the dialogue for the pope is the encounter in the present between the churches and "today's people of the covenant concluded with Moses." Note again the pope's insistence on the church's acceptance of the continuing and permanent election of the Jewish people. Such a notion calls for Christian appreciation of Judaism's own self-definition and for an awareness that the church has a very real stake in the survival and prosperity of the Jewish people today.

This second dimension, which the pope terms "a reciprocal learning process," obviously will entail a full-scale engagement of people on all levels of our respective communities, from the local to the international. Here, I believe, is where the uniqueness of the American experience can make a significant contribution to the endeavors of the universal church and world Jewry. Not only is America blessed by being able to count the world's largest Jewish community among its citizens, but its history of pluralism has provided a fit setting for contacts and cooperation all through our shared history on these shores. The Catholic and Jewish Communities in this country have undergone common immigrant experiences and developed remarkably similar patterns of coping with the problems of assimilation and nativist rejection. Such shared experience and common commitment to pluralism provides a solid foundation for further sharing today.

The national workshops on Christian-Jewish relations (the sixth of which will take place in Milwaukee Oct. 26-29, 1981) thus reflect in the diversity and range of topics discussed the manifold concerns of our two communities. We will need to develop ever better educational tools and sources if the fruits of such dialogues are to be passed on to succeeding generations of our youth.

3. The third dimension of dialogue suggested by the pope is oriented from the present into the future. Here, he urges our attention to ''the tasks that we have in common...to work jointly for peace and justice'' in the world. Such joint social action as understood by the pope is not merely a secular enterprise but a properly religious one, a ''holy duty.'' The pope thus finds its source deep within the biblical tradition, in the call to Abraham ''to be a blessing for the world'' (Gn. 12:1).

Again it is good to be able to note the many steps already being taken in this counrty to live up to the concreteness of this challenge. Our conference has cooperated with Jewish agencies on a variety of programs, from migration services to action for Soviet Jewry to educational efforts aimed at the elimination of prejudice. Joint or parallel statements on the important social issues of our times continue to mark our cooperative efforts. The ongoing discussion of the religious foundations of social policy in the Catholic and Jewish traditions, sponsored by ourselves and the Synagogue Council at the University of Notre Dame (and aided by a National Endowment for the Humanities grant), have been especially important in achieving the understanding necessary for successful cooperative action.

We do not, of course, always agree on social matters. But we have shown an ability to continue to dialogue despite such differences as, for example, in the meetings held between the Synagogue Council and ourselves concerning abortion over the past several years.

Finally, running through the three-dimensional pattern of dialogue as sketched by the pope, I believe is a sense of hope, one might even say of eschatological longing. This is the longing for the kingdom of God, whose vision we share. Such a vision can provide us with a proper goal for the endeavor of dialogue as a whole. In the perspective of the kingdom we can find a sense of common witness, a witness to the world by Jews and Christians together. In this perspective, past practices of false proselytism are eschewed in favor of a deeper awareness of the nature of our mission.[1] As the pope comments: ''In all this it is not only a question of correcting a false religious view of the Jewish people, which caused, in part, the misunderstandings and persecution in the course of history, but above all a question of the dialogue between the two religions which, with Islam, can give to the world the belief in one ineffable God who speaks to us and... the entire world.''

The pope, who began his talk with a poignant reference to the Holocaust,[2] ended with a moving tribute to Israel, ''this unique land visited by God...the land to which all Jews look with special reverence.''[3] This statement recalls that made by our own conference in 1975:

''Jews have explained that they do not consider themselves as a church, a sect or a denomination as is the case among Christian communities, but rather as a peoplehood that is not solely racial, ethnic or religious, but in a sense a composite of all these...Whatever difficulties Christians may experience in sharing this view they should strive to understand the link between land and people which Jews have expressed in their writing and worship throughout two millenia as a longing for the homeland holy Zion" (NCCB, Nov. 20, 1975). We have, after all, been listening and learning in dialogue. I can only pray that such mutual cooperation will continue. Linked together in the perspective of the past which calls us into being and of the future which gives us our destiny, Catholics and Jews can today work and dialogue together as never before in all the ages of our often troubled yet still common history.

1. For a fuller study of this question, see T. Frederici, "Study Outline on the Mission and Witness of the Church," presented to the International Vatican-Jewish Liasion Committee Meeting in Venice, March 28, 1977, published in SIDIC journal (Vol. 9:3, 1978) 25-34, and Origins (Vol. 8, 1978) 273ff.

2. The pope's compassionate understanding of the tragedy of the Holocaust was clearly revealed in his pilgrimage to Auschwitz in 1979: "I am here today as a pilgrim. It is well known that I have been here many times. So many times...among the ruins of the crematorium furnaces...I kneel on this modern Golgotha of the modern world, on these tombs largely nameless like the great Tomb of the Unknown Soldier. I kneel before all the inscriptions that come one after another bearing the memory of the victims of Oswiecim (Auschwitz)...In particular I pause with you before the inscription in Hebrew. This inscription awakens the memory of the people whose sons and daughters were intended for total extermination...It is not permissible for anyone to pass by this inscription with indifference" (Origins, June 2, 1979).

3. In his homily at Otranto the pope specifically linked the Holocaust with the rebirth of the Jewish state of Israel. This is the strongest expression to date of papal recognition of the support for the moral legitimacy of Israel, a fact largely overlooked in the controversy over the second portion of the statement, which some have construed to be a vindication of certain Palestinian claims. "The Jewish people, after tragic experiences connected with the extermination of so many sons and daughters, driven by the desire for security, set up the state of Israel." (L'Osservatore Romano, Oct. 13, 1980).

DATE DUE

HIGHSMITH   #LO-45220